IRONMAN'S

ULTIMATE GUIDE TO
ARM TRAINING

Also in the *Ironman* series:

Ironman's Ultimate Guide to Natural Bodybuilding
Ironman's Ultimate Guide to Bodybuilding Nutrition
Ironman's Ultimate Guide to Building Muscle Mass
Ironman's Ultimate Bodybuilding Encyclopedia

IRONMAN'S

ULTIMATE GUIDE TO
ARM TRAINING

IRONMAN MAGAZINE **AND PETER SISCO**

Contemporary Books

Chicago   New York   San Francisco   Lisbon   London   Madrid   Mexico City
Milan   New Delhi   San Juan   Seoul   Singapore   Sydney   Toronto

Library of Congress Cataloging-in-Publication Data

Ironman's ultimate guide to arm training / Ironman magazine and Peter Sisco [editor].
      p.   cm. — (Ironman series)
    Includes index.
    ISBN 0-8092-2815-7
    1. Bodybuilding.   2. Arm.   I. Title: Ironman's ultimate guide to arm training.
II. Sisco, Peter.   III. Ironman (Marina Del Rey, Calif.)   IV. Series.

GV546.5 .I772   2001
646.7'5—dc21   00-52382

Contemporary Books

A Division of The McGraw·Hill Companies

1 2 3 4 5 6 7 8 9 0 VL/VL 0 9 8 7 6 5 4 3 2 1

ISBN 0-8092-2815-7

This book was set in Minion by Hespenheide Design
Printed and bound by Vicks Lithograph

Cover design by Todd Petersen
Cover photograph copyright © Michael Neveux. All rights reserved.
Cover model: Todd J. Smith

McGraw-Hill books are available at special quantity discounts to use as premiums and sales promotions, or for use in corporate training programs. For more information, please write to the Director of Special Sales, Professional Publishing, McGraw-Hill, Two Penn Plaza, New York, NY 10121-2298. Or contact your local bookstore.

This book is printed on acid-free paper.

CONTENTS

FOREWORD

Ironman magazine was founded in 1936 by Peary and Mabel Rader of Alliance, Nebraska. Their first print run of 50 copies was done via a duplicating machine that sat on their dining room table. *Ironman* started out as an educational vehicle to inform and enlighten those people who were interested in weight lifting, bodybuilding, and, eventually, power-lifting.

The focus of *Ironman* magazine during its first 50 years was on all three sports, with emphasis on weight training in general as a life-enhancing activity. *Ironman* has always stressed the health and character-building aspects of weight training and has always been the leader in bringing exercise and nutrition concepts and ideas to those in the training world.

In the early '50s, *Ironman* magazine was the first weight-training publication to show women working out with weights as part of their overall fitness regimen. It even went so far as to show a pregnant woman training with weights and educating readers on the benefits of exercise during pregnancy—thoroughly modern concepts 25 years ahead of their time. In the late '50s and early '60s, *Ironman* magazine was the first to talk about high-quality proteins derived from milk and eggs as well as liquid amino acids. The bimonthly magazine had, by this time, acquired over 30,000 subscribers simply on the strength of its informa-tion. The Raders never worked at expanding its circulation. It grew by word of mouth fueled by the general hunger for and *Ironman*'s ability to provide intelligent, timely, and reliable training information.

By the early '80s, the Raders, now in their 70s, had spent nearly 50 years working incredibly long hours to put out a bimonthly publication. The hard work was beginning to take its toll.

I'd been interested in *Ironman* as a business since the mid-'70s and had in fact talked several times with the Raders about purchasing *Ironman*. Eventually, my dream of owning and publishing a bodybuilding magazine was realized, and in August 1986, after 50 years, *Ironman* magazine changed owners. At that time, *Ironman* had a circulation of 30,000 subscribers, had no foreign editions, was published bimonthly, and averaged 96 black-and-white pages, with a color cover. Fifteen years later, *Ironman* magazine is published worldwide with an English-language circulation of 225,000 and additional editions in Japanese, Italian, German, Arabic, and Russian.

The books in the *Ironman* series represent the "best of the best" articles from more than 60 years of *Ironman* magazine.

John Balik
Publisher, Ironman

ACKNOWLEDGMENTS

I would like to thank the following people who made this book possible:

John Balik, publisher of *Ironman* magazine, had the foresight to see the need for this book and the others in the *Ironman* series. His knowledge of bodybuilding and his sensitivity to the information required by readers has made *Ironman* the best bodybuilding magazine in the world.

Steve Holman, editor in chief of *Ironman*, creates one informative, insightful issue of the magazine after another, and his own articles in this book show ample evidence of his innovation and encyclopedic knowledge of the iron game.

Mike Neveux is the premier bodybuilding photographer in the world. His photos in this book and in every issue of *Ironman* magazine have inspired and motivated countless bodybuilders around the world by capturing the intensity, power, and magnificence of these great athletes.

A special thanks to Terry Bratcher, art director of *Ironman*, who did an enormous amount of work in the preparation of this book by wading through *Ironman*'s immense archive of articles and photographs in order to help bring you the "best of the best."

Finally, I would like to thank all the writers who contributed to this book. These writers have an incalculable collective knowledge of the sport of bodybuilding. This book represents the distilled knowledge of hundreds of man-years of study in every aspect and nuance of the iron game. Between the covers of this book are wisdom and experience that would cost a small fortune to obtain from one-on-one training with these writers. It is the thought, effort, and writing of these individuals that make this book and *Ironman* magazine great.

Peter Sisco
Editor

Part I

COMPLETE ARM-TRAINING WORKOUTS

Bill Pearl.

Chapter 1

BILL PEARL'S ARM-BUILDING SECRETS

BY GENE MOZÉE

I first saw Bill Pearl compete in the '53 Mr. Southern California contest. He was an unknown at the time, having done all his training at Leo Stern's gym in San Diego. Pearl decimated the precontest favorites—Zabo Koszewski, Joe Baratta, and Dom Juliano—winning the title as well as the Best Arms, Best Legs, and Most Muscular awards. Six weeks later, he returned to the Embassy Auditorium in Los Angeles, the scene of the first contest, and won the highly coveted Mr. California title. Two months after that, he won the AAU Mr. America. Shortly thereafter he flew to London, where he won the amateur Mr. Universe crown.

When you consider that he won them all on his first try, Pearl's clean sweep of four major titles in one year has never been duplicated. In his final competition 18 years later, he defeated all of the top bodybuilders in the world—Reg Park, Sergio Oliva, Frank Zane, Serge Nubret, Franco Columbu, and Dave Draper—with the exception of Arnold Schwarzenegger, who declined to enter because he was obligated to compete in the IFBB Mr. Universe, which was held one week later. Pearl had issued a challenge a year before the contest to every bodybuilding superstar on planet Earth to compete against him at the NABBA Mr. Universe in London on September 17, 1971. Only Arnold was a no-show. In the estimation of many bodybuilding authorities, this was the greatest muscle contest ever held.

When Bill Pearl won the Mr. America in '53, he weighed 202 pounds. When he won his final Mr. Universe in '71, he weighed 242 with laser-sharp definition. It was just one month before his 41st birthday.

In my opinion, Pearl deserves to be heralded as the greatest physique champion of all time. In 18 years of major competition, he was beaten only once, in 1956, when he overconfidently entered the Mr. Universe and didn't even shave his chest and lost the Overall to Jack Delinger. Pearl did win the Mr. Universe Tall Class at that contest, however. His total of five Universe titles and his unmatched record of longevity as a world champion rank him number one in my book. What other champion has been at the top for 18 years? None. Case closed.

Pearl opened his first gym in Sacramento, California, in 1954. The tremendous training knowledge he gained during his years under

Leo Stern's guidance enabled him, in turn, to begin cranking out northern California bodybuilding champions such as Don Farnsworth, Al Souza, Walt Horton, and future America and Universe winner Ray Routledge.

In 1962 Pearl sold his Sacramento gym and moved to Los Angeles, where he purchased the George Redpath Gym and started producing local champions such as Jerry Roquemore, Mike Barnett, and Jerry Wallace. World power-lifting champion Pat Casey, the first man to officially bench-press 600 pounds, trained at Pearl's gym, along with world shot put record-holder Dallas Long and many University of Southern California football all-Americans, including Mike Henry, who later starred with the Green Bay Packers and Los Angeles Rams. Henry also became a movie star; he made three *Tarzan* pictures and is probably best remembered as Jackie Gleason's sidekick in several *Smokey and the Bandit* movies.

In the mid-1960s Bill opened his famous gym in Pasadena, California, where he proceeded to turn out Mr. America and Mr. Universe winners such as Chris Dickerson, Jim Morris, and David Johns. He also helped several other physique stars, including Dennis Tinnerino, Boyer Coe, and Tony Pearson. Bodybuilders from all over the world flocked to Pearl's facility for his specialized training techniques and his inspiring guidance. Rory Leidelmeyer, a superstar of the 1980s, received his first professional training advice from Bill Pearl.

Pearl's physique was famous for its total development; from the ankles to the neck, no muscle was incomplete. His arms, in particular, were acknowledged to be among the greatest of all time because the biceps, triceps, and forearms were massively developed from all angles. Pearl was one of the very first men to appear on stage with an arm that was legitimately 20 inches cold. What's more, his fabulous physique and legendary arms were built without steroids or muscle-enhancement drugs of any sort.

I interviewed Pearl about his arm training at his Pasadena gym. Although it was many years ago, the techniques he revealed to me at

Pearl's physique was famous for its total development.

that interview will work just as well today if not better because of the improved nutrition practices now being used. Here's how he described his program.

According to Bill Pearl:

"Big arms dominate the thoughts of all bodybuilders. I've had more requests for advice on arm training than any other body-part. I'm going to tell you about a terrific mass-building program that also builds shape and cuts. It not only works for me, but I've also given it to many of my pupils, and they've made excellent gains on it.

"I train my arms three times a week. On those days, I do abdominals first, as a warm-up, then move on to back, arms, and calves. On my other three workouts, I do abs, shoul-

ders, pectorals, thighs, and calves. In other words, I do abs and calves at every workout.

"I've tried every known arm-training technique. I've always done arm exercises that enabled me to use heavy poundages. For triceps, for example, I was never much for repetition dips or bent-over kickback exercises and preferred heavy dumbbell triceps extensions, heavy barbell curls, and lying triceps extensions. I felt I got better results from heavy poundages. The lighter stuff was OK for pumping and shaping, but it didn't trigger the growth factor. I have always handled as heavy a weight as I could in the strictest style."

TRICEPS

"I always begin my arm workouts with triceps. Of all the muscle groups, I think I enjoy train-ing biceps the least, and I tend to do things I like best first, which I admit isn't always a good idea. Nevertheless, working triceps is more enjoyable for me, and I can handle very heavy poundages. It gets my arm workout off to a good start."

These are the exercises:

Barbell or dumbbell triceps extensions

"I use both hands, keep my elbows in close to my head, let the weight go all the way down behind my neck, and lock out my arms at the top. I do all reps as strictly as possible—5 sets of 6 with all the weight I can handle."

Lying barbell triceps extensions

"With my head off the edge of the bench and my chin up, and using a close grip, I lower the bar to my chin, then return to the fully locked-out position. I prefer to isolate the triceps action by using a grip that's six to eight inches wide. By doing the movement strictly, I elimi-nate the necessity of using excessively heavy weights, and that's helped me avoid injury as I lower the bar to my chin and push straight up.

I use about 135 pounds now but have used as much as 185. I do 5 sets of 6 very strict reps."

Lying dumbbell triceps extensions

"Using one dumbbell while lying on a flat bench, I lower the weight to the opposite side of my head. I keep the upper arm vertical by gripping the biceps with my free hand. I use a 60-pound dumbbell for 5 sets of 6 reps, alternating the right and left hands without resting."

Reverse-grip bench presses

"I use a fairly close grip on these. I lower the weight to just below the lower-pec line and then press it all the way up and fully lock out my elbows. I do 5 sets of 6 strict reps."

BICEPS

"After completing the heavy triceps workout, I go on to biceps." Here are the exercises.

Seated dumbbell curls

"While seated on the edge of a flat bench, I curl two dumbbells together until they touch my delts. I use a back support and keep my elbows close to my sides, with the dumbbell turned out. Using strict style, I do 5 sets of 5 reps. I follow this immediately with light reverse-grip triceps pressdowns or leaning triceps pushups for 15 reps. That allows me to keep the pump in my triceps while blasting my biceps. I do a set of one of those light triceps pump movements after completing each biceps exercise. They are easy movements, and you don't have to set up for them; so, you don't waste time."

Lying barbell preacher curls

"I perform these while lying facedown on a bench. This truly isolates the biceps and builds thickness in the lower portions. I do 5 sets of 5 reps." [Note: This is similar to a spider curl.]

One-arm concentration curls

"I do this one while seated. I don't like to do it while standing, because of the tendency to hump the weight up and cheat the reps. I keep my free arm away from my leg and do 5 sets of 6 reps in strict style, curling the weight to my deltoid rather than to my chest."

Standing barbell curls

"Using a shoulder-width grip, I do 5 sets of 6 reps. I may go as low as 5 reps but never fewer than that. I can go as high as 8, but if I'm handling heavy weights, I don't like high repetitions, because I get more fatigued mentally than physically. I can't keep myself geared up through a set of high, heavy reps. When I was

Bill Pearl built arms that measured 20 inches—cold—using all natural methods.

a kid, I could do anything, but I'm not up to that now. I grow better on lower reps."

Here's the complete routine.

BILL PEARL'S FORMULA FOR BIG ARMS

Triceps

Barbell or dumbbell triceps extensions	5 × 6
Lying barbell triceps extensions	5 × 6
Lying dumbbell triceps extensions	5 × 6
Reverse-grip bench presses	5 × 6

Biceps

Seated dumbbell curls	5 × 5
Reverse-grip pressdowns or leaning triceps pushups	1 × 15
Lying barbell preacher curls	5 × 5
Reverse-grip pressdowns or leaning triceps pushups	1 × 15
One-arm concentration curls	5 × 6
Reverse-grip pressdowns or leaning triceps pushups	1 × 15
Standing barbell curls	5 × 6
Reverse-grip pressdowns or leaning triceps pushups	1 × 15

The preceding program is for advanced or competitive bodybuilders. Here's a program for less advanced and noncompetitive bodybuilders.

NONCOMPETITOR ARM BLAST

Pushdowns	3 × 10
Lying triceps extensions	3 × 8
Parallel bar triceps dips*	3 × 10–12
Barbell curls	3 × 8
Incline dumbbell curls	3 × 8
Standing dumbbell curls	3 × 8

*Can also be performed between two benches.

ARM-BLASTING TIPS

"No matter which program you use, you'll find the following suggestions helpful for building big arms.

1. Do all the exercises as strictly as possible. Don't cheat.
2. Use a weight that allows you to get a complete extension and contraction on each rep.
3. Concentrate on the area you're working, and train at a speed that will keep it warm. With a little experimenting, you'll find the pace that's best for you.
4. Don't forget about weight progression. The following system works best for me: Take, for example, pushdowns performed on the lat machine. Let's say you start with 60 pounds and do 3 sets of the required repetitions. I'd use the same weight for the first three workouts. On the fourth workout, I'd do 2 sets with 60 pounds and 1 set with 70 pounds. On the fifth workout, I'd do 1 set with 60 pounds and 2 sets with 70, and on the sixth workout, I'd do all my sets with 70 pounds. Use the same progression system from then on, as long as you can do the reps strictly.

   Remember, however, that these are just sample poundages. Use the weights that are best suited to your ability and strength. Just be sure to start fairly light so that you can do all of the exercises correctly.
5. Keep a daily record of the weights you use on each exercise, and always keep a positive attitude about your workouts."

Darin Lanaghan.

Chapter 2

COMPOUND AFTERSHOCK ARM TRAINING

BY STEVE HOLMAN

Are you looking for a training routine that will inflate your arms to eye-popping proportions in record time—a program based on scientific principles and exercise analysis so it absolutely, positively can't fail? Then you've come to the right article. After only three workouts with the following Compound Aftershock routine, your arms will feel fuller than ever before, and with some diligent effort you'll eventually look as if you have 20-pound hams stuffed in your shirtsleeves—or perhaps 15-pounders, depending on your genetics.

How much discomfort must you endure for this transformation to occur? Well, the routines do require a high pain threshold, but the entire program takes less than 15 minutes.

We all need a little convincing before we start a new program, so here are the reasons this science-based arm program produces such spectacular results:

1. **It uses the most effective exercises**. According to the book *Muscle Meets Magnet* by Per A. Tesch, Ph.D., which takes an MRI [Magnetic Resonance Imaging] look at which parts of leg and arm muscles are hit hardest by certain exercises, the movements in the Compound Aftershock superset hit the target muscle structures completely, rather than focusing on certain heads.

■ **Decline extensions.** This exercise puts maximum stress on the lateral, long, and medial heads of the triceps. You get total target-muscle stimulation with one efficient exercise. According to *Muscle Meets Magnet*, lying extensions on a flat bench, the most common version of this exercise, somewhat neglect the lateral and medial heads and focus on the long head. If you want to totally torch your tri's, do your extensions on a decline.

■ **Overhead dumbbell extensions.** This exercise also puts maximum heat on all three triceps heads when you use two dumbbells. The same movement done with a bar instead of dumbbells ignites only the lateral and medial heads, leaving the long head lagging behind. The reason the dumbbell version may be more effective is that your palms are facing each other. MRI analysis proves that varying your grip can have a substantial effect on target-muscle stimulation, as you'll see with the biceps exercises as well.

- **Close-grip barbell curls.** This exercise puts a total hit on the medial and lateral heads of the biceps. The brachialis muscles even get complete stimulation. If you do the exercise with a wide grip, however, MRI analysis says the medial head, the one closest to your torso, takes the brunt of the stress, and the lateral head and brachialis lag behind. Keep your grip close on curls, about 10 inches between your hands, and you'll get a more complete overall biceps hit.

- **Incline curls.** Once again, you sledgehammer the medial and lateral biceps heads. The unusual stretch you get on this exercise may be the reason. Keep your feet firmly planted on the ground, curl the dumbbells simultaneously, and don't pause at the bottom—change the dumbbells' direction immediately once you reach the complete stretch position, to activate the myotatic reflex.

Incline dumbbell curl—midpoint.

Overhead dumbbell extensions.

Concentration curls.

Close-grip barbell curls.

Mohamed Makkawy.

2. **The myotatic reflex, or prestretch, helps max out fiber recruitment.** This is especially true when you place the stretch exercise before a big midrange movement in a superset. For example, you can superset incline curls with close-grip barbell curls. Let's go through the entire Compound Aftershock biceps routine so you can see exactly how and why it's so effective.

Decline triceps extensions.

Close-grip barbell curls.

- After a couple of warm-up sets, you train the mass of the muscle with a heavy set of close-grip curls to failure. Muscle synergy from your front delts makes this heavy overload possible.
- After a brief rest, you move to the Aftershock superset. First you use incline dumbbell curls to trigger the myotatic reflex for some extraordinary fiber recruitment—a call to arms for the reserve fibers. With a preponderance of fibers in a heightened state, you immediately follow up with a lighter set of close-grip curls—about 20 percent lighter than your first set—so that synergy once again forces maximum fiber recruitment.
- After a two-minute rest and some massaging of your incredibly pumped biceps, you finish them off with concentration curls, 1 or 2 sets, squeezing hard for a count at

the top of each rep for a peak-contraction effect.

Your biceps can't help but grow after this on-target attack. Triceps get the same treatment:

■ Do 1 set of decline extensions. It's OK if your upper arms move so that you get some synergy from your lats and teres muscles; just don't overdo it.

■ Rest for a minute as you decrease the weight on the bar, then do 1 set of overhead dumbbell extensions supersetted with a second set of decline triceps extensions with the reduced poundage. Your triceps fibers will be screaming for mercy and pumped to the bursting point.

■ Rest for about two minutes, and notice how your tri's are so full that

Incline dumbbell curls.

Triceps kickbacks.

they feel as if they're a couple of inflated tire tubes hanging from your rear delts. Now finish them off with dumbbell kickbacks, making an effort to get your upper arms back past your torso on every rep as you contract your triceps hard. One set of this peak-contraction pain is all you have to endure—2 if you're a real masochist.

3. **Better pump and burn.** New research suggests that supersetting helps lower the blood pH, which can force more growth hormone release. These findings may verify why bodybuilders have been instinctively chasing the pump for years. It may be a growth stimulus after all.

4. **Brachialis work for higher peaks.** The brachialis runs under the biceps, and when you develop this muscle, it can give your bi's more height, much as a developed soleus gives the lower legs more fullness. While close-grip barbell curls put a lot of stress on the brachialis, you may want to do 1 direct finishing set to give it that extra jolt. *Muscle Meets Magnet* says incline hammer curls, with your thumbs up and palms facing each other, provide a focused hit on the brachialis.

5. **More recovery for accelerated growth.** You stimulate each target muscle to the maximum with only 4 or 5 sets, which means you have more recovery ability left for hypertrophy. Remember, the more sets you do, the more you deplete your system's ability to recover from intense exercise, so efficiency is key. Obviously, this is one heck of an efficient arm-building program because you fatigue as many fibers as possible with as few sets as possible.

How should you use the Compound Aftershock arm routine for best results? An every-other-day split is the program that will help most intermediate bodybuilders make the best gains. Here's a sample:

Workout 1
Quads, hamstrings, calves, chest, and triceps

Workout 2
Back, delts, biceps, and abdominals

Always take a day of rest between workouts, and you have a recovery-oriented split that will produce impressive size increases.

If you prefer full-body workouts, a different approach is necessary, as follows:

Monday

Squats	2 × 8–10
Leg extensions	1 × 8–10
Leg curls	2 × 8–10
Standing calf raises	2 × 12–20
Seated calf raises	2 × 12–20
Bench presses	2 × 8–10
Pulldowns	2 × 8–10
Bent-over rows	2 × 8–10
Dumbbell upright rows	2 × 8–10
Full-range crunches	2 × 8–10

Wednesday
Compound Aftershock arm routine—you may want to do 2 supersets instead of only 1, since you have more time to recover—or any arm-specialization program.

Friday
Same as Monday

With this program, you train arms only once a week, on Wednesday, with the full Compound Aftershock routine. Consequently, you may be able to get away with a few more sets, such as doing 2 supersets instead of 1, but keep in mind that biceps and triceps get indirect stimulation on Monday and Friday from the pressing, rowing, and pulldown movements. This indirect work will pump blood into your arms for heightened recovery, but you want to make sure you don't overtrain. You'll see impressive results from this type of program in a matter of weeks, guaranteed.

If buggy-whip arms is the disease, Compound Aftershock is the cure. Give this routine a try, and watch as your bi's and tri's swell to hamlike proportions in record time.

Vince Comerford.

SEVEN TIPS FOR MASSIVE ARMS

1. When you train triceps and biceps on the same day, always do triceps before biceps. Pumped bi's can reduce the triceps' ability to reach a full stretch on certain exercises. For example, with pumped biceps you tend to stop short on overhead extensions, which can diffuse the stretch reflex.

2. If you work arms along with other bodyparts, train them at the end of your routine. The indirect work from presses, pulldowns, and rows will help warm up your arms and prime them for the direct work to come.

3. Always work your brachialis—either with a specific exercise, such as incline hammer curls, or with a direct biceps exercise that also focuses on this muscle, such as close-grip barbell curls. See *Muscle Meets Magnet* for other suggestions.

4. Use supersets periodically. You can achieve more growth hormone release, a more extensive capillary network, and more muscle-fiber stimulation with this stress technique.

5. Eat some protein and carbohydrates every three hours. This keeps the muscle repair process in motion, stuffs the bi's and tri's with glycogen for more volume, and prevents catabolism. If you don't eat every few hours, your body can cannibalize hard-earned muscle tissue.

6. Keep your form ultrastrict on all exercises except those on which you want synergy, such as decline extensions and close-grip barbell curls. Those movements should be done with slightly looser form to bring muscle teamwork into play so that more target-muscle fibers will be stimulated.

7. Don't overtrain. Remember that your biceps and triceps get hit hard during presses, rows, pulldowns, and chins. Keep that in mind when constructing your arm routine. Doing fewer sets for arms is usually the best strategy when you're not specializing on arms.

Paul DeMayo.

COMPOUND AFTERSHOCK ARM ROUTINE

Triceps

Decline extensions*	1 × 7–9

Aftershock superset

Overhead dumbbell extensions	1 × 5–7
Decline extensions	1 × 5–7
Kickbacks	1–2 × 7–9

Biceps

Close-grip barbell curls*	1 × 7–9

Aftershock superset

Incline curls	1 × 5–7
Close-grip barbell curls	1 × 5–7
Concentration curls	1–2 × 7–9

Brachialis (optional)

Incline hammer curls	1 × 7–9

*Do 1 or 2 light warm-up sets before your work set.

Rob Colacino.

Chapter 3

ROB COLACINO'S ONE-REP-PER-BODYPART TRAINING

BY DAVID PROKOP (COLACINO PHOTOS BY JERRY FREDERICK)

Dorian Yates, Mike Mentzer, Arthur Jones, and all you other famous and not-so-famous proponents of high-intensity training: step aside, please. Make way for the man who's truly taken high-intensity training to the ultimate conclusion.

He's Rob Colacino, a 5'9½", 245-pound bodybuilder from East Haven, Connecticut, and the current NABBA Mr. U.S.A. Perhaps you've never heard of Rob before, but that's about to change. Once you learn how this dedicated 31-year-old muscleman trains, chances are you'll never forget him.

What Rob does is unique; he's never heard of anyone else doing it—and neither have we. His approach is not for the weak of heart or soft of gut. It works for him, though, and he has the muscle to prove it, including the kind of freaky mass that had the late Don Ross so excited that he was planning to write several articles on Rob.

The man himself talked to us while cradling his infant daughter, Kaylee May, in his mighty arms as his wife, Kimberlie, looked on, during a recent visit to California.

"I don't really worry about measurements. I just get as big as I can. But my arms have been measured at 22 inches. No bull. Cold even. And, yeah, my arms get a lot of attention—but so do other parts of my body.

"Let me tell you, I train everything hard. I put everything into it. It's as if I never have a

One rep done so slowly that it looks like an isometric rep.

bad workout. I train everything to the extreme.

"And I have some very specific ideas about training. First of all, the bigger I've got, the less I train, but the more intensely I train. So, it's less volume but more intensity.

"Take, for example, a biceps workout. There are weeks when I may train a little differently, but the majority of the time, I train biceps once a week, and my entire biceps workout consists of 1 rep. Not 1 set, but 1 rep. This is no exaggeration; I did it in the gym this week. One rep a week. I've cut it down to that.

"Of course, there's warming up. I don't train every bodypart like that, but I work the majority like that.

"So, if I'm training biceps, I do incline dumbbell curls, my favorite exercise. And I do 2 warm-up sets with a light weight, no more than 6 to 8 reps, but I don't tax myself. Then I grab very heavy dumbbells—I've gone up to 105 pounds. I start moving the weight up from the bottom, going real slow. I stop in the middle and hold it there for as long as I can; I stop and hold it on the positive, and I also hold it on the negative.

"So, what we're talking about here is a very *l-o-n-g* rep. It could go on for minutes. At the top, I do little squeezes. And when I go back down, I do it very slowly. Again, I'll stop and hold it on the negative as long as I can. When I get to the bottom, I try to go back up—I try and I try, until I just can't budge the weight anymore. Then I know that the muscle has had it, that I've gone to failure. It's 1 rep, but it's heavy and so intense. You wouldn't believe the sweat that's pouring off me.

"I do two exercises for triceps: usually an overhead rope extension and a rope pressdown, 1 rep for each exercise, in the same way I do the biceps exercise, holding on the positive and on the negative. And at the bottom after completing the rep, I'm not giving up right away but trying to get it back up, even though there's no way I'm going to do it because the muscle has already been pushed to the limit.

"For chest, I mainly do 2 exercises, flat bench presses and incline bench presses, the same way: 1 rep per exercise. Sometimes I do flyes for chest. I warm up with a couple of light sets, and then I do 1 rep, going up very slowly, then stopping and holding it on the positive and also on the negative. Then at the end of the rep, I keep on trying until I just can't budge it anymore, and I know I'm dead and I've failed.

"For back, I do chins, same way. T-bar rows, the same way. But on bent-over rows, I do sets of 6. I go up 5 pounds every week; I'm up to 405 pounds for 6. Next week I'll do 410. The next week I'll do 415, hopefully.

"I don't do a pressing movement for shoulders when I've done bench presses,

because I feel my front delts are already hit. So, I do a side lateral with dumbbells—1 rep again, holding it on the positive and on the negative. And then I go down, and I try to do another rep, but I just can't. I train the rear delts the same way. I do the rear delt machine, kicking it back.

"For traps, I do 1 rep on shrugs, although sometimes I do heavy shrugs for 6 reps.

"How long could I extend a single rep of this type? I've had my partner look at the clock, and I've held an incline dumbbell curl on the way up for about a minute and a half or two minutes. I've actually done that, but it's crazy. That's intense! Usually I count to 50 in my head or something like that.

"If you were to watch me do a single rep like this, it may almost look as if it's an isometric contraction, but there's movement—very slow, but there's movement.

"In an exercise such as the bench press, I'll stop the movement a good three-quarters of the way up. I'll stop it there for however long my mind lets me, and however long I think it's good, and then I just inch it slowly up all the way and lock out. I come back down; I stop at

the same point, hold it there for as long as I can, bring it down as slowly as I can, let the bar touch my chest, then try my hardest to bring it back up just to make sure I'm dead.

"If I've done the rep to my maximum, there is no second rep. There can't be. But I try to get a second one just to make sure I've had enough.

"I have people spotting me on each side of the bar on bench presses and in the middle. I tell these people, 'Don't touch it until I tell you.' I know it's on my chest, and I know I'm not moving it, but I'm doing this for a reason. It's hard to find people I trust to spot me. With the bench presses, you need a good spotter or two; otherwise, you won't get the bar off your chest.

"I used to train the same way as everybody else—you know, 4 to 5 sets per exercise, 10 to 12 reps per set. In '94 I started training only four days a week with weights—working each bodypart once a week, doing low sets—and I started thinking, 'Geez, if I'm growing now, why don't I just get more rest but train much more intensely?' In other words, train harder and get more rest—at the same time. I wanted

training, and he said, 'It sounds as if you've brought Mentzer's training to another level. To the ultimate conclusion.'

"Mike Mentzer was one of my early idols, and I have the utmost respect for him. But I do feel I've taken it to another level.

"I know bodybuilders who are doing 16 to 20 sets per bodypart, and I guess it works for them. But no matter how great they may look, I think they could be even better if they trained the way I train."

Robbie is quick to point out that while he generally does this type of training for his upper body, he follows a more traditional approach when training legs. For example, he does 4 sets of 6 to 10 reps on squats. He tries to add 5 pounds per week on his last set. He was doing 585 when he visited California, and he planned to do 590 the next week, 595 the week after that, and so on.

The only leg exercises on which he does the 1-rep style are leg extensions and hamstring curls. He doesn't do 1 rep when training abs either; he works his abs four days a week, using various forms of crunches.

to take my training somewhere that it hadn't been before.

"I had been doing, say, 10 reps, and on the 10th one, I would hold it—the way I'm doing now. And it suddenly dawned on me: 'Why do the other 9?' Just hold it on the first rep, when I'm actually at my strongest.

"I didn't work down gradually, from 10 to 5 or 4. I just went right down from 10 reps to 1, thinking, 'I'm going to do only 1 rep, but I'm going to make this 1 rep so intense and make it last so long that at the end of that rep, the muscle will be wasted.' I just knew it would work. And it did.

"Obviously, it's patterned after Mike Mentzer's Heavy Duty. He talks about taking intensity to the extreme by doing 1 maximal set. What I've done is actually take it one step further by doing 1 maximal rep.

"Ed Corney was head judge at the '94 NABBA U.S.A., when I finished second overall. He freaked out when he saw me. Then, of course, in '95, he was there again, and I was even better. He freaked out again and took me out to dinner afterward. I told him about my

Robbie's weekly training schedule is as follows:

Monday
Off

Tuesday
Chest and triceps

Wednesday
Shoulders and biceps

Thursday
Off

Friday
Back and traps

Saturday
Off

Sunday
Thighs and hamstrings

He typically does aerobics four days a week, but he increases it to five and then six days a week before a competition.

"The mind-set is very important because you really have to be into what you're doing: that 1 rep has to be it. If you don't do it well, you're not doing anything.

"What drives me crazy is that I never think I did that 1 rep hard enough. You may see me in the gym dying, but in my mind I'm thinking, 'Damn, I didn't do it well enough.' I think that's what makes me train harder every workout.

"Your mind has to be able to take the pain, and it has to be able to overrule the objections of the body, because your body doesn't want to hold that rep. It wants you to finish the rep; it doesn't want to hold it. It doesn't want you to try to get the weight up again for a second rep.

"Actually, you're battling the muscle and the mind at the same time. I have a training partner who says, 'Rob, this is almost 90 percent mind.'

"In a workout like this, the weight you use doesn't really matter, although I always go as heavy as I can. To some extent, I'll vary the

weight—sometimes going heavier, sometimes lighter.

"My top poundages are something like 105 for incline dumbbell curls, 375 for bench presses, and 330 for incline bench presses. For dumbbell flyes, I've gone up to 140s, but I've also gone as low as 80 and [extended the rep]. For dumbbell laterals, I use 40s and 50s.

"You've got to keep in mind that doing an exercise such as the bench press for 1 hold-it rep is a whole lot different from doing 1 or 2 regular reps. For one thing, you're not using momentum.

"When you train like this, as opposed to doing a regular workout, the feeling you have is that the muscle is burned. It hurts so much. I always concentrate on doing that 1 rep to the very best of my physical and mental ability. I must put all my effort into it, and it's so intense that I almost get scared before the workout. When I was doing 10 to 12 reps, I would warm up and then do 6, 8, 10, 12 reps for several sets, and that was it. Now I know that 1 rep is all I've got.

"You know, when you're doing 10 to 12 reps in an exercise, the first 6 to 8 reps of each set feel fairly easy, and there's not very much discomfort. It hurts only on the last few reps. So, in the earlier reps, it's almost as if your muscle is getting a break. When you do 1 rep like this, it's going to be uncomfortable right from the very beginning.

"To motivate myself to the maximum, I may think of things to get me really mad or think of somebody saying I'm not good enough or whatever. When you're doing that 1 rep, the feeling is just pain, but it's fun. I love it at the end when I can't even move the weight. I feel as if I've reached my goal. It's hard to explain the feeling.

"This is the way I'll always train. Of course, it takes some getting used to. We're accustomed to moving the weight at a normal speed. When you start going very, very slowly, the body just doesn't want to do it. It wants to take advantage of momentum, get the rep over faster.

"But it's exciting to me. It's certainly a challenge. You talk about strict, controlled exercise form with continuous tension: could anything be stricter and more controlled than this? I love it.

"When I tell people what I'm doing, they're skeptical. They're like, 'I've got to do 10 sets for biceps. I can't do 1 rep!'

"Well, all right. I've got 22-inch arms. Go ahead and do 10 sets, and have your 15-inch arms.

"They just don't believe it. They just don't think it can work. Plus they don't know how to do 1 rep, either. They would have to do it with me to really understand it.

"At the same time, even though it's a very demanding way to train, the workout is short. That counterbalances it a little.

"I've been asked whether I would recommend that a teenager or someone just getting started in bodybuilding do this type of training. My answer is no. I think you really have to build a strong foundation before you're able to handle this type of training mentally and physically. This is a very advanced form of training.

"This is a very hard way to train. This is taking it to the limit. This is taking it to a level that scares people off. I have people who are too scared to train with me—and these are guys who compete."

Sergio Oliva.

Chapter 4

SERGIO OLIVA'S SATURATION BOMBING ARM ROUTINE

BY GENE MOZÉE

Sergio Oliva is a bodybuilding phenomenon. He was the first muscular giant to appear on the scene with incredible size and laser-sharp definition—and legitimate 21-inch arms. In 1967 he gave the bodybuilding world a historic 21-gun salute while winning his first Mr. Olympia title. The legendary Bill Pearl said, "Sergio was ahead of his time. That thin-skinned, vascular, highly defined look wasn't in vogue until Sergio arrived." That's probably because no one had ever before reached Oliva's level of massive, striated muscularity combined with near perfect proportions.

I've seen many bodybuilders who had sensational arm development. Back in the 1950s there were the fabulous arms of Marvin Eder, Bob Shealy, Joe Sanceri, Babe Stansbury, Steve Reeves, Clancy Ross, Jack Delinger, Malcomb Brenner, and Reg Park. All of those stars had arms that measured 18 to 19 inches in peak contest shape.

In the early 1960s Freddy Ortiz (19½ inches), Larry Scott (20¼), Dave Draper (20½), and Bill Pearl (20½) were the reigning kings of arm size and muscularity, but in 1967

Sergio Oliva topped them all when his fabulous guns extended the tape measure to a full 21½ inches. Not only were his arms huge, but they were also ripped to shreds with dazzling definition and deeply chiseled separation. His arms were totally developed from the deltoid to the elbow. They were wide, full, and thick from every angle. In fact, I've never seen anyone whose arms were as impressive as Sergio's were when they were hanging at his sides relaxed. His triceps development was arguably the greatest ever.

Remember that Sergio reached this milestone in bodybuilding history before the arrival of human growth hormone and the sophisticated injectable steroids that are available to modern muscle stars. It's a good thing, too, in my opinion. Sergio and the other superstars mentioned did it with hard work and good nutrition.

Look at the champions of the past who continued to compete or give posing exhibitions for 20 or more years: Pearl, Park, Scott, Serge Nubret, Lou Ferrigno, Albert Beckles, Frank Zane, and Robby Robinson. Sergio—a

Larry Scott and Freddy Ortiz, circa 1960s, in front of the historic Vince's Gym, Studio City, California.

study in bodybuilding longevity—has been at the top, or nearly so, for 30 years! Today's champs seldom last longer than 10 years. Steroid burnout? I think it's more than a possibility.

During the many opportunities I had to observe Sergio train at the legendary Vince's Gym in Studio City, California, when he was visiting the West Coast for posing exhibitions,

I was able to gain valuable insight into his training methods. His concentration was so intense that he never spoke to anyone during his workout, except maybe a few words to Vince Gironda. After he finished working out, however, he was quite gregarious and displayed a great sense of humor. He would answer questions about his training thoroughly. One time, he described the program that built those 21-inch-plus arms.

When Sergio began training in his native Cuba in 1960, his arms were only 13 inches. At that time, he was an Olympic weight lifter and did only exercises that would build strength for that sport. Even so, his arms grew rapidly and were 17 inches when he reached a bodyweight of 198 pounds.

After defecting to the United States in 1962 and eventually settling in Chicago, he began bodybuilding at the Duncan YMCA. Although his arms were large and full, they were not very shapely, lacking a good biceps peak and sweeping triceps. He also needed

Concentration curls.

Triceps pressdowns.

sharp separation between the individual muscles and much greater definition.

"Size alone is not everything," explained Sergio. "When I won the Junior Mr. America title in 1966, I had built my arms up to 19 inches. My arm size increased to 20 by the time I won the Mr. World contest. But when I say that arm size isn't everything, here is a perfect example. In my first try for the Mr. Olympia crown, I was defeated, and I am sure that incomplete arm development—regardless of how massive my arms were—cost me the title."

Sergio was criticized at the time because his physique lacked separation, even though he was in top shape, without an ounce of fat. "So unanimous was the criticism that I had to completely reassess my development," he said. "It was then that I realized I had to discard all the training techniques I had been using and find new ones that would be more effective."

He started studying all the training methods of the champions and reading everything he could find on arm training, seeking the answer to the problem of increasing shape and definition. He eventually incorporated many of those ideas into his own unique system.

Barbell curls.

Reverse barbell curls.

"Most bodybuilders think that just the biceps and triceps form the total upper arm," Sergio stated. "Not true: the brachialis underlies the biceps and inserts near the elbow. This muscle is essential, for without its full development the elbow area looks weak and underdeveloped."

Sergio went on to explain that the brachialis is brought into use during curling and reverse curling movements. "It can be especially developed by the reverse curl—an exercise that I have always included in my workouts. Look at any of my arm poses, and you can clearly see the brachialis development.

"You should consider the upper arms as being composed of three muscles: the biceps, triceps, and brachialis," Sergio continued, "and each must be fully developed if you want the acme of arm development. That is how I got my arms up to 21½ inches."

Sergio used two particular techniques to the fullest to blast his arms past the 21-inch barrier: supersets and superconcentration. It's

Scott curls on machine.

one thing to perform supersets—quite another to perform them with the utmost concentration. He favored supersets because they are a time-saver that enabled him to get more into—and out of—his workouts. "They make it possible to attack my arms more fiercely, giving them a saturation blitz that brings an ultimate pump and forces them to grow larger and more defined more rapidly," he emphasized.

Sergio considers concentration to be the "true key to success in bodybuilding," he said. "I am convinced that without concentration, you can't develop a championship physique." He further stated that without concentration, your physique will be incomplete and not symmetrical. "Therefore, I work hard and force every rep of every set, all the while concentrating to the limit of my capability. I keep my mind focused directly on the actual

movement of the weight—on the exact muscle being worked and on the correctness of my form."

Sergio credits the combination of supersets and maximum concentration with adding the size, shape, and separation that enabled him to win the Mr. Olympia title in 1967. "I can't stress the importance of concentration too much," he said. "Keep a constant reminder in your gym or locker with a sign that says 'Concentrate.' If you're preoccupied with other things, your workout will be largely wasted. And talk *after* your workout—not during it."

Sergio trains his arms twice a week, on Tuesday and Saturday. Other than a warm-up superset for the abdominals, he devotes the entire workout to his arms. Here's the routine. It takes him about two hours and is made up of just 5 supersets.

SERGIO OLIVA'S SATURATION BOMBING ARM ROUTINE

Superset 1: For Mass

Standing barbell curls	5 × 8
Reverse barbell curls	5 × 15

Superset 2: For Full Development

Scott curls on machine*	5 × 8
Standing barbell extensions	5 × 8

Superset 3: For Mass and Power

Lying barbell extensions	5 × 8
Standing dumbbell extensions	5 × 8

Superset 4: For Biceps Shape and Cuts

Seated dumbbell curls	5 × 8–10
Dumbbell concentration curls	5 × 10

Superset 5: Finishing Triceps Pumper

Pressdowns	5 × 10
Reverse pressdowns	5 × 10

*Sergio used the Scott curl machine at the Duncan YMCA, rather than the usual Scott curl bench, but you can get the same terrific benefit with either piece of equipment.

SERGIO'S ARM-TRAINING TIPS

1. This program is for only very advanced veteran bodybuilders, and even they should break into it gradually. It's definitely not for beginning or intermediate trainees.

2. Use strict form on all exercises so that the target muscle gets the total benefit of the movement. Keep your body movement to a minimum at all times.

3. If you're really advanced in arm work, don't stop after 5 complete supersets of the Scott curls–and–standing extensions combo, Superset 2. Instead, decrease the weight on both exercises by 20 pounds and do 3 supersets, increasing the reps to 10. Also, do them a bit faster than the first 5 supersets. This saturation blitz really pumps the arms to the maximum.

4. Handle as heavy a weight as possible on all exercises, but don't sacrifice form for poundage. Always strive for a complete range of motion on every movement.

5. For Superset 4, keep your body perfectly still on both exercises, and use very strict form. Concentrate intensely on the action of the biceps, and cramp and tense them at the top of the curling movement.

6. On the pressdowns, always make sure that your body is solidly planted, that only the triceps work, and that you apply equal pressure with both arms.

7. Superset 5, the finishing triceps pumper, not only ensures you of a massive pump, but it guarantees complete development as well.

8. If you want maximum gains, concentrate on every rep of every set of every exercise.

9. Make sure you get lots of rest and sleep, and don't participate in any fast-arm sports such as tennis or golf.

10. Eat a well-balanced muscle-building diet that includes plenty of protein from meat, fish, eggs, cheese, and milk. Be sure to eat only the best

fresh fruits and vegetables for the natural carbohydrate energy you need for heavy training.

11. Stay away from junk foods and highly processed foods, which are practically useless for building muscle size.

12. Don't do more than two arm workouts a week on this arduous program. Three will be too much, and not only will you burn out quickly, but also you may even get smaller.

"If you are ready for it," said Sergio, "this program can take your arms from 17 or so inches at the start and blast them into 20-inchers and beyond—and maybe, someday, all the way to the Mr. Universe and Mr. Olympia titles!"

Will Willis.

Chapter 5

SMART ARM TRAINING WITH WILL WILLIS

BY RUTH SILVERMAN

"I've finally got smart," declared WNBF pro Will Willis. The drug-free bodybuilder was talking about his decision to open a private training gym, but he might well have been talking about his arm training over the years. When it comes to loading the guns he displayed in winning the '93 ABCC Natural California and taking second at the '94 WNBF

Dumbbell preacher curl—start.

Dumbbell preacher curl—finish.

Concentration curl—start.

Mr. Universe, he said, "I know that my arm workouts in the beginning were a lot longer than they are now.

"I was like a lot of people—you have a strong bodypart, you want to train it all the time," continued Willis, who also admitted,

"I was flexing my biceps way back in elementary school." His genetic predisposition for big arms got a considerable push during his teenage career in gymnastics, during which he won the Montana state championship on the parallel bars in his sophomore year in high

Concentration curl—midpoint.

in 1983 and who responded to the constructive criticism by limiting his arm training for a full year. He'd been working arms twice a week. He cut back to once a week, if that, doing maybe 3 light pumping sets for each bodypart for maintenance. He focused on bringing his chest and back into balance and figured his bi's and tri's were getting plenty of indirect work.

Eventually he switched to competing in the AAU and returned to blasting his arms. He was preparing for national-level competition and "wanted to be as extremely built as possible." The result was a string of victories culminating with a win at the '87 Mr. U.S.A.

Standing barbell curl—start.

school. "Everything you do in gymnastics pretty much involves triceps," he observed. "My biceps grew from all the iron crosses, and triceps from all the parallel bar and pommel horse work."

Consequently, when he started weight training during the summer before his senior year, it wasn't long before he was doing 15 to 20 sets each—as many as 4 or 5 exercises—for biceps and triceps. He trained that way until he was 21, when after-the-show conversations with bodybuilding judges wised him up to the fact that he was starting to look like Popeye.

"Symmetry is my thing now," explained Willis, who was the NPC Regional Teen Bodybuilder of the Year in northern California

Standing barbell curl—finish.

Barbell preacher curl—start.

Willis dropped out of bodybuilding competition and stopped weight training seriously for a couple of years in the late '80s, a period of personal growth during which he became very involved in his church. He started training clients—and training for competition again—in 1991, earning pro status in the WNBF, which requires athletes to be drug-free for at least seven years.

Although his main focus these days is getting Ironwill Private Training off the ground, the 5'11", 193-pound Willis is in shape year-round for modeling jobs and never far from contest condition. "You get me on a little bit of phosphagen and a few weeks of hard training, and I'm ready to compete," he said. "I'm a little tighter than what I was before. I've got a 29-inch waist. My chest still measures 49, so I've got a 20-inch difference . . . [and my biceps are] taping at 18½, which is pretty good for a natural guy."

Veteran bodybuilding photographer Russ Warner once compared Willis's rear double-biceps to that of Arnold Schwarzenegger

Barbell preacher curl—finish.

Seated triceps extension—start.

Seated triceps extension—finish.

"because I have the five different heads that lead up to that peak at the top."

Nowadays Will hits his biceps and triceps on separate days once a week as part of a four-days-on/three-off schedule. Here's his body-part split:

Day 1 Chest and biceps

Day 2 Legs and calves

Day 3 Back

Day 4 Shoulders and triceps

With his busy schedule of training clients, Willis does his own weight workout in the evening. He does abs and cardio on days 1 and 3 in the morning and engages in some form of heavy cardiovascular activity, such as in-line skating or mountain biking, on two of his off days.

In his bodypart routines, Willis likes to rotate exercises; for example, he breaks up a couple of sets of alternate dumbbell curls with a set of concentration curls. He also likes to do what he calls pyramiding down in weight. After the first heavy exercise, on which he goes up in weight and down in reps, he often does the opposite—starts with his heaviest weight and works up in reps.

WILL BUILDS BICEPS

Lately, Willis has been organizing his biceps workout around preacher curls. "Those seem to peak my biceps," he said. "They hit the outer head really well. They hit the inner head at the top of the movement. I get a good stretch on the outer head at the bottom. I keep my elbows in real tight, and I get a real good peak when I hit a full contraction."

As part of his maintenance program, Willis alternates heavy and light weeks on

biceps training, but he goes heavy on the barbell preacher curls even on his light week.

A typical Will Willis biceps workout starts with a few light sets of standing barbell curls. "I don't do those heavy anymore, because my back can't take it," he said, but they make a great warm-up. He does 6 to 7 work sets for biceps on day 1 after performing 12 to 15 sets for chest.

Here's a typical program for his heavy week. For his light week, he does 20 to 25 reps on 2 sets of concentration curls and rotates them with 1 set of down-the-racks on the alternate dumbbell curls.

WILL'S BICEPS BLAST

Warm-up

Standing barbell curls	2 × 15–20
Dumbbell curls	1 × 15–20

Work Sets

Barbell preacher curls	3–4 × 4–8

Rotate Exercises*

Alternate dumbbell curls	2 × 10
Concentration curls	1 × 20

*One set of dumbbell curls, followed by concentration curls, followed by the other set of dumbbell curls.

WILL TRAINS TRICEPS

For this muscle group, Willis favors seated one-arm dumbbell extensions, as well as seated barbell extensions, on which he brings the bar back behind his neck. "I get the best stretch on my triceps with those particular exercises," he observed.

"I really don't do a lot of close grip, because the outer part of my triceps is really well developed. I think that sometimes if you're too developed in that area, it takes away from the look of the arm."

For triceps work, he also sticks with 6 to 7 work sets, which come on the heels of 12 to 15 sets for shoulders.

Here's a typical heavy-week workout:

Lying triceps extension—start.

WILL'S TRICEPS TOASTER

Rotate Exercises*

Seated one-arm dumbbell extensions	3 × 20, 15, 10
Pressdowns or lying triceps extensions	2 × 10–12
Seated barbell extensions**	2 × 8–10

*One set of one-arm dumbbell extensions, followed by a set of pressdowns, followed by a set of one-arm dumbbell extensions, etc.

**Behind the neck.

A ROUTINE FOR ALL SEASONS

Willis generally starts his clients out on higher reps and not so many sets for arm training. Aside from beginners, however, he believes the preceding routines "would be good for anyone who wants to build as well as maintain, and for anyone who's on drugs or off drugs," he said. The lesson he learned about arm training seems to be the trend, he observed. The results of his less-is-more approach are hard to miss.

Lying triceps extension—finish.

"I've been looking at other natural body-builders. I think our bodies are a little more worn," he added. "We've already got ourselves to the optimum level, where we don't need to be in the gym for two or three hours a day to reach the kind of goals we did when we were younger." One thing Will Willis has learned throughout his training days is, he gets the same effect after an hour and 15 minutes of training as he got two years ago—as relative to even eight years ago—after three hours of training.

Cable crossovers.

Chapter 6

MASS RULES
SEVEN BOOSTERS THAT CAN BUILD MUSCLE 10 TIMES FASTER

BY STEVE HOLMAN

For most people, building muscle is harder than negotiating peace in the Middle East. Yet, we see reports of spectacular, sometimes unbelievable, progress—in the area of muscle growth, that is, not Middle Eastern peace initiatives (where bombing and blasting have much scarier meanings). Take Casey Viator and the Colorado Experiment back in 1973. With Nautilus creator Arthur Jones hovering over his every workout with a menacing look in his eye—according to some sources, Jones was also frequently armed with a revolver—Viator managed to pack on an incredible 60 pounds of muscle in four weeks. His achievement was the result of only 12 high-intensity workouts that had an average length of less than 30 minutes each, which was the very reason *Ironman* used the Colorado Experiment workouts as a model for the Phase 1 program in 10-Week Size Surge.

Keep in mind, however, that Viator was rebuilding muscle size after a layoff from competitive bodybuilding. Nor can you forget the inspiration provided by Jones's packing heat, not to mention Viator's awesome genetics at the ripe old age of 22. The man was the quintessential mesomorph and had won the Mr. America when he was only 19. Genetics and firearms aside, though, that's quite an accomplishment, especially when you consider that it takes most trainees about 40 workouts to add 1 pound of muscle.

You read that right. Forty grueling workouts for 1 measly pound of muscle. Now, that's phenomenally inefficient. If those results are the norm, is it any wonder that so many people quit bodybuilding?

If you've fallen into that kind of rut—or been in one ever since you started training—never fear. Here are seven critical rules to remember to make sure you're getting the absolute most hypertrophic stimulation out of every single session.

DECREASE THE MOMENTUM, INCREASE THE GROWTH

Every time you hitch, jerk, or bounce a weight, you lose valuable muscle-building resistance.

Decrease momentum, increase growth.   Bruce Patterson.

EMG/force-plate studies have shown that if you press a barbell rapidly, you'll actually lose tension on your deltoids through part of the range of motion—the part right after the bounce. For example, a 60-pound barbell, if pressed suddenly with a jerk, can exert a force of several hundred pounds or a force that measures below zero, depending on where along the muscle's range of motion the measurement is taken. The reason is inertia. You have to heave a fairly heavy weight to get the bar moving rapidly, and while that can be advantageous under controlled conditions in some forms of strength training—for example, in properly applied plyometrics—if you're trying to build muscle size, you want to keep tension on the target throughout its range of motion. Strive for a two-seconds-up/two-seconds-down cadence—or more time on movements that have a longer stroke, such as squats—even if you have to count out loud, "one-thousand-one, one-thousand-two." That will better stimulate the target muscle along the entire length of its fibers and provide a more appropriate time under tension for growth stimulation, although it will make your grueling squat sets last longer. (Tip: Picture Jones and his revolver to help get you through it.)

SUCK IT IN, FORCE IT OUT

You've seen it hundreds of times: trainees holding their breath during exertion. That's not a good idea. For one thing, you could black out, fall face-first into the dumbbell rack, and end up with "40 lbs." imprinted backward on your forehead. From a muscle-building standpoint, when you're driving up heavy poundage, you want to keep all systems primed and running smoothly so that you can regenerate ATP, the muscles' energy compound, and get every last rep possible. In other words, you don't want to starve your system of oxygen (passing out can really drain your motivation). The rule is: Breathe in on the negative, or the easier part, of the rep, and breathe out on the positive, the more difficult part. On the squat, for example, breathe in on the way down, and blow out as you drive the weight up. You may hold your breath for a second or two as you reverse directions, but exhale as you hit the hard part of the rep. A forcible outflow of air can focus your power and give you a burst of strength. It's the reason martial artists tend to *kiai* [yell] as they punch and kick—to focus their *chi*, or body energy. Warning: Don't do a screaming *kiai* on every rep, or your gym membership may be revoked, not to mention your reputation for sanity.

CIRCULATE THE AMINOS, ACCELERATE GROWTH

Most bodybuilders know to eat some protein every two to three hours to keep their muscles bathed in amino acids. You don't want the starvation mechanism to kick in and cause your body to start cannibalizing its muscle tissue for energy—unless you're going for that Gandhi-on-a-hunger-strike physique. Did you

Suck it in, force it out.

Circulate aminos, accelerate growth.

know, however, that when you eat solid food, it may take as long as 45 minutes before digestion breaks down the protein into aminos, the building blocks of muscle, and gets them into your system? If your last meal was three hours earlier, you may be on the verge of tripping the catabolic switch. With another 45-minute wait, those important ounces of biceps muscle you stimulated during your last few arm workouts may get burned for energy.

The answer is to drink a small protein shake with meals, or swallow some amino acid capsules about 15 minutes before you eat. That will ensure that your bloodstream is flooded with those anabolic catalysts right away, and the aminos from the solid food will follow soon thereafter. If you go the drink route, a casein-and-whey combination is perfect because you get a fast anabolic effect from the whey as it enters your bloodstream almost immediately and a slow, trickle-feed effect from the casein that can keep you in a positive nitrogen balance for hours.

AVOID THE PAIN, MISS THE GAIN

OK, so it's just a rewording of the famous bodybuilding credo "No pain, no gain," but it rings true, especially when you're talking exercise selection. Many trainees go the easy route and pick isolation movements. Watch some of those male-model types train in the gym, and you'll see them doing leg extensions, lateral raises, and machine curls. About the only compound movement they do is bench presses, which may explain why so many male models have big pecs but small—albeit defined—quads, delts, and biceps. They base their workouts around easy isolation exercises, usually on machines.

Granted, the big, compound movements are hard as hell, but while they do create more pain, they also initiate more gain, probably because you can use more poundage when a number of muscle structures work together. Teamwork allows for more overload and activates the mass of the fibers in the target muscle. If you want more size, use a compound exercise as the core of each bodypart routine.

Avoid the pain, miss the gain.

STRETCH FOR SIZE

A number of experts have touted the effectiveness of stretching to enhance muscle size. The theory is that stretching can make the fascial encasements around muscle fibers less constricting, so growth comes easier—but who the hell has time to do a stretching program and work out? The answer is to incorporate stretch-position movements into every bodypart routine. That means you not only train every muscle with progressive resistance but also work it against resistance at the point at which it's maximally elongated. Examples of stretch-position exercises include stiff-legged deadlifts for hamstrings, flyes for pecs, sissy squats for quads, and pullovers for lats. For an added fascial-expanding effect, hold the stretch on your last rep for 8 to 10 seconds—at the bottom of an incline curl, for example.

Stretch for size.

Another reason to incorporate stretch-position movements is the possibility of hyperplasia, an increase in the number of muscle cells—more fibers equate to more growth capacity. While the phenomenon hasn't been proven to exist in humans, an animal-based study that was published in the journal *Medicine and Science in Sports and*

Exercise showed that muscle-fiber hyperplasia does occur due to "stretch overload" (25:1333–45; 1993). Scientists also believe that stretching a muscle both increases the number of anabolic receptors on it and initiates the release of good prostaglandins, which can enhance muscle growth tremendously. In other words, stretch-position exercises can provide the new pain that can ramp up your gains.

HOLD THAT CONTRACTION

Forcing your muscles to contract against more and more resistance is the essence of building more size, so why not emphasize the peak contraction of exercises that have resistance in the contracted position? For example, when you do undergrip pulldowns, cable crossovers, or lateral raises, you have to fight to hold the weight in the contracted position because there's resistance. Hold for at least a count to get maximum fiber stimulation and an extra jolt of anabolic stress.

If you really want to emphasize the contraction, try static-contraction, or X-Rep, training. As I reported in "Underground Mass-

Boosting Methods," an informal study (Sisco and Little, *Static Contraction Training*, Contemporary Books, 1999) proved that holding a weight and contracting against resistance until failure has phenomenal size-and-strength repercussions. One subject gained 28 pounds of muscle in 10 weeks using that method exclusively, and another gained 3.75 inches on his chest.

If you want to try it, simply pick a weight that you can hold for 20 seconds in the strongest position along an exercise's stroke. Gradually increase your hold time at each workout until you can hold the weight for 30 seconds, then up the poundage at your next workout to bring your hold time back down to 20 seconds. Progressive resistance coupled with maximum contraction is the key. Try it on one set of a few exercises in which there's resistance in the contracted position, such as at the top of a leg extension or leg curl, and see if you don't get a surge of new growth.

BURN, BABY, BURN

European researcher Michael Gündill reported in the August '97 *Ironman* that muscle burn is directly related to increases in growth hormone release. One of the studies that verify his findings was published in the *Journal of Strength and Conditioning Research* (10:256–62; 1996). It involved exercise and growth hormone release, and the results suggest that when the blood pH is lowered through exercise, it causes acidic buildup, and more growth hormone is released. Other studies have made that correlation as well.

It means that you should strive for a pump and burn in every bodypart at every workout, which is the basic premise of Compound Aftershock training. The strategic supersetting of two exercises for the same bodypart is a proven trigger for growth. Of course, you can also get that burn by using straight sets, but if you ever find yourself at the end of a bodypart routine and you haven't achieved a pumped, burning sensation, add one last set, and make it a descending set. Pick

Hold that contraction.

Burn, baby, burn.   Bruce Patterson.

a weight that will allow you to get about 5 perfect reps. When you hit failure, decrease the weight, and immediately crank out another set to failure. When you hit failure on your second set—probably around rep 4 or 5—decrease the poundage one last time, and rep out. That's another great aftershock technique, and if you don't have that pumped, burning feeling before you complete one of those intense triple-drop torture-tactic sets, you will afterward.

Another bodybuilding benefit of maximum pump and burn is the development of capillaries, which adds to muscle size, makes the muscles more efficient at performing work, and can give you a more vascular appearance when you're lean. (Every bodybuilder knows that when people see veins, they always ooh and aah about what great shape he or she is in.)

Integrating the seven critical mass boosters into your training and diet can do wonders for your muscle growth. You may not gain 60 pounds in 12 workouts as Casey Viator did thanks to Arthur Jones and the Colorado

Feel that burn!

Experiment, but, then again, do you really want to train under the gun—and have to worry about someone's popping a cap in your ass at every workout? It makes a lot more sense to follow the seven critical rules, not to mention fewer gym fatalities.

Part II

FOREARM TRAINING

Figure 7.1.

Chapter 7

STANDING WRIST CURLS

BY JOSEPH M. HORRIGAN, D.C.

Forearm exercises seem to go into and out of vogue, sometimes due to the forearm development of popular bodybuilders and their descriptions of their training for that bodypart. Some bodybuilders and power lifters develop significant forearm muscles from their back and arm training and don't train their forearms at all. Others have to work at forearm development.

Most trainees who have had injuries that required a visit to the doctor have heard the advice "Stop training." It's one of the most devastating comments a trainee can hear, and it frequently comes from doctors who have little or no weight-training background. While continuing on the path of exercises that produced the injury is certainly folly, there may be ways to work around it, stabilize the joint or anatomical structures that have been injured, and prevent a flare-up or worsening of the problem.

In Chapter 12, I discuss the hammer curl as an alternative for those who have wrist pain and injuries. Here the topic is the standing wrist curl. Many trainees develop wrist pain

Figure 7.2.

Figure 7.3.

from their occupations, their sports, accidents, or perhaps even their training. Such injuries can include arthritic wear and tear through the small bones of the hand (metacarpals) or the long bones of the forearm (radius and ulna). Ligaments of the wrist can be torn or overstretched, and trainees may have surgery on them. The ligament-and-cartilage complex in the wrist, known as the triangular fibrocartilage complex (TFCC), is commonly torn. One carpal, known as the scaphoid, or navicular, is the most commonly fractured bone of the wrist and can produce lifelong problems.

As you can see, many problems can occur in the wrist that would necessitate strengthening the area. What do you do if the common exercises for the wrist, such as wrist curls and reverse wrist curls, produce pain? There are alternatives—exercises that can be used both by people who have injuries and by those who are healthy but simply wish to try something different. The standing wrist curl fills that need.

The '97 NABBA Mr. Universe class winner, Frank Vassil, demonstrates the exercise under

discussion. The photos were taken at the Daniel Freeman Hospital Center for Athletic Medicine in Manhattan Beach, California.

In Figures 7.1 and 7.2, Frank performs the standing wrist curl, and as you can see, he takes a close grip on the bar and holds it behind his back. The distinct advantage of the exercise is evident in the bottom position, where the wrists are straight. At the bottom of a standard wrist curl, where your forearms are on a bench or on your thighs, your wrists are bent at approximately a 70-degree angle (see Figure 7.3). That can place too much force on your wrists and produce pain or aggravate an injured or unstable wrist. The standing wrist curl doesn't produce the same stress. There's usually little, if any, pain in the bottom position for trainees who experience pain when they perform regular wrist curls.

The compression of the wrist joints is reduced when you do standing wrist curls, so you can try to wrist-curl the bar as high as reasonably possible. If the top of a standing wrist curl produces pain, you can try to stop the movement a few degrees short of full range of motion, which may alleviate the pain.

The flexor muscles of the wrist have both long and short components. The long muscles of the forearm that flex, or bend, the wrist originate on the inner part of the elbow, which is known as the medial epicondyle, so they actually cross the elbow. The short muscles originate along the long radius and ulna. When the wrist is fully flexed during the finish of a standing wrist curl, the flexor muscles are performing a significant amount of work. The full extent of this advantage is not yet known.

The first time I saw the standing wrist curl used as a regular part of a training program was in 1974. Enrique Hernandez, the world power-lifting champion in the 132-pound class, included forearm training as part of his bench-press program. Enrique believed that strong forearms helped support the weight when he benched. I don't know if there's any validity to that idea, and no one else does either. All that exists are theories. Fifteen years ago, I worked for a physical therapist who was a 220-pound power lifter. He scoffed at Enrique's idea.

We don't know if Enrique had elbow problems. We can theorize that if the ligaments on the inner side of his elbow (ulnar collateral ligaments) were overstretched or loose and caused the elbow to move too much (valgus laxity), then the forearm strengthening would have provided added support for the elbow, which could have made him feel more secure and strong when he was benching. Again, this is all theory, as neither the physical therapist nor I ever examined Enrique's elbows.

Enrique included several sets of wrist curls, standing wrist curls, and reverse wrist curls at the end of his bench-press workout. If you think his technique will be beneficial for you, try it. You should start any new exercise carefully, using low sets and reps to avoid causing a new injury or aggravating an old one.

It's certainly possible to develop significant strength in your forearm muscles. I've seen a number of bodybuilding champions using 135- to 185-pound barbells and 130-pound dumbbells on wrist curls. If you look through old issues of *Ironman, Muscular Development,* or *Strength and Health,* you will find articles about a man named Slim-the-Hammerman. I don't recall his last name, although I'm sure some readers will remember him. Slim-the-Hammerman used to perform various feats of strength with sledgehammers and with sledgehammers that had weights attached to them. He'd place his forearms across an anvil and, using wrist strength alone, move the weighted sledgehammers in various directions. Champion wrist and arm wrestlers have told me of performing dumbbell wrist curls with 150- to 220-pound dumbbells.

In the past, I wrote about a patient who had the largest forearms I've ever seen. I've had the opportunity to treat people who were known for their forearm development, such as Dave Draper and the Barbarian brothers. This particular patient was 6′6″, weighed 350 pounds, and had forearms that—measured with a steel tape—were 19¼ inches. His name was Mac, and those who trained at his gym will remember him. He performed wrist curls with 315 pounds for 5 reps. After I wrote that, I received several pieces of mail from readers who noted that it was impossible for someone to have forearms that big. I know how they feel. I've been around this game a long time and been to the most famous gyms in the western United States. I've heard plenty of nonsense stories about how big some people are or how much they allegedly lift. There are a lot of tall tales out there, but this isn't one of them.

This patient entered an over-40 physique contest in which the last pose requested by the judges was a forearm shot. When he heard that request, the man knew he'd won.

If you're working around a wrist injury, the standing wrist curl is an excellent choice for training your forearms with little—or decreased—pain. It's also a good exercise for healthy trainees. As I've said before, train smart first, and then train hard. If you do, you may not have to worry about working around so many injuries.

Chapter 8

FREAKY FOREARMS

BY DAVE TUTTLE

There's no question that superior forearms are an essential part of trophy-winning arms. While most bodybuilders put primary emphasis on their biceps and triceps, the forearms make up a substantial portion of total arm size. Starting at the wrist, where they have a circumference so small that you can wrap your fingers around them, the forearms increase in size until the girth below the elbow is at least twice that of the wrist. This exploding forearm mass makes your arm development even more impressive when you do a double-biceps pose.

Despite this fact, many bodybuilders neglect their forearms. Some athletes forget to do forearm exercises entirely, while others occasionally throw in a single forearm movement when they have time or energy left over after their biceps or triceps workout. While this hit-or-miss approach may have been sufficient in the past, today's level of physique competition demands a more exacting strategy.

If you want to develop an extraordinary set of arms, you need to think of your arms as a combination of three bodyparts instead of the traditional two. While biceps will always remain the king of bodyparts, and shredded horseshoe triceps will continue to make the judges sit up and take notice, only those bodybuilders who combine awe-inspiring forearms with superior biceps and triceps will get the recognition when it comes time to hand out the awards.

THE FUNCTION OF THE FOREARM MUSCLES

The forearm region contains an unusually large number of muscles. Each finger is connected to a forearm muscle and tendon, which enables it to move independently. Additional muscles move the hand as a whole and rotate, raise, and lower the forearm. To see what a complex part of the body it is, position your forearm parallel to the floor in front of your body. Now move each finger, and see how your forearm changes in shape. Making a fist and

Reverse curl—start.

Reverse curl—finish.

rotating it toward the forearm moves the forearm mass toward the elbow, much as flexing the elbow pushes the biceps muscle into the peak we all know and love.

There are a total of 20 muscles in the forearm. Most of them originate on the humerus, or upper-arm bone, although a few originate on the radius or ulna, which are the two bones of the forearm. Nearly all of the muscles insert in the wrist or hand regions, depending on their particular function, although four insert above the wrist.

NOVICE WORKOUT

Athletes who have not done forearm exercises in the past should begin with the novice workout. This routine introduces you to the rigors of forearm training without demanding so much effort that you strain the muscles. Your drive for superior forearms begins with a single exercise:

Seated dumbbell
wrist curls   3 × 6–10

Always start with a warm-up on this and every exercise, using 40 percent of the weight you'll lift on your 3 main sets. This is important because each exercise works the muscles differently. Try to do at least 6 reps per set, and focus on progressive resistance. When you can do 10 reps with a given weight, increase the weight. That will temporarily lower the number of reps you can do, but over time you'll gain strength and get up to 10 again. Keep repeating this process, and watch as your forearms balloon in size.

BEGINNING-ROUTINE EXERCISES

Seated dumbbell wrist curls

Select a dumbbell that's approximately half as heavy as the one you use for biceps curls. Straddle the middle of the bench, and sit down. Place the dumbbell in one hand, and lean forward, resting your forearm across the width of the bench (or on your thigh), with

Seated dumbbell wrist curl—start.

Seated dumbbell wrist curl—finish.

your wrist floating in the air just off the edge of the bench and your palm facing up. You should be leaning far enough forward that your trunk is almost parallel to the bench.

Gripping the dumbbell tightly, lower your hand to fully extend the wrist. Now slowly flex the wrist until your knuckles are visible. In this position, the forearm is completely contracted. Hold this position for a second, and crunch the muscle. Return to the starting position, and repeat. When you've done the specified number of repetitions, change hands, and repeat with the other forearm.

If you find that you're stronger in one forearm than the other, start with the weaker forearm. Continue to alternate arms as indicated. Force out as many repetitions as possible with the weaker arm, and then stop with the same number of reps on your stronger arm—even if you could do more. In time, this should reduce the strength differential between your two forearms so that they'll become equally massive.

INTERMEDIATE-ROUTINE EXERCISES

Once you master the novice workout, you can move on to the intermediate routine. This one piles on the intensity with a second exercise.

Reverse curls with wrist flexion

This exercise is often used as a supplemental movement for the upper arm because it recruits the brachialis and biceps muscles. It also involves the brachioradialis and other forearm muscles that are used in elbow flexion, and performed as described here, it works the muscles that flex the wrist as well.

Select a barbell that's a moderate weight for your strength level. Take a shoulder-width overhand grip. Your hands should be in a straight line with your forearms. Slowly raise the barbell until it's approximately even with your chest. Do not move your upper arm. As you lift the barbell, let your hands drop so that they're no longer in line with your forearms. Your knuckles should face forward at all times. At the top of the movement, your wrists should be fully flexed and all of your forearm muscles contracted. Hold for one second, then lower the barbell to the starting position. Repeat for the specified number of repetitions (see page 71).

ADVANCED-ROUTINE EXERCISES

Competitive bodybuilders can achieve ultimate forearm mass and shape with the advanced workout, which adds a third exercise to really blast the target muscles.

Seated barbell wrist curls

This exercise can produce killer forearms when done properly. Frequently it's performed with the fingers tightly gripped around the bar at all times, similar to the seated dumbbell curl. To make your forearms burn to the point where they cry out for mercy, however, you modify the exercise by allowing the barbell to roll down to your fingertips. The incredible stretch this creates and the full-length contraction produced afterward, when you make a fist, will stimulate some real size gains.

Because of its difficulty, you should perform this exercise with a relatively light weight, at least initially. Select a barbell, and place it in front of one end of a bench. Sit, straddling the middle of the bench. Then lean forward, with your forearms parallel to each other so that they rest on the bench's padding and your wrists float in the air just beyond the edge of the bench above the barbell, with your palms facing up.

Now that you know the correct position, stand, and pick up the barbell with your palms facing forward. Your hands should be no more than two inches apart so that both forearms can rest comfortably on the bench. Sit on the bench again, and move into the proper position. Slowly open your fists, and let the barbell

roll down your palms. When it has almost reached your fingertips, reverse the momentum of the barbell by curling your fingers into a fist again. Flex your wrists until the knuckles are visible. Hold for a second, then repeat.

FINISHING OFF THE FOREARMS

One of the best ways to finish off a muscle is to do a movement that isolates a specific action. In the case of forearms, that means squeezing. After you've blown out your forearms with wrist curls and reverse wrist curls, pick up a Super Gripper and squeeze out as many reps as you can with each hand. After that, move on to isometric squeezes. Pull the hand grips together, and hold for 20 to 30 seconds. Do this for each hand.

Why does the Super Gripper work so well? Because it provides your muscles with an essential ingredient for awesome size and strength: specificity. That means the Super Gripper mimics the gripping action exactly so that the neurological pathways and specific muscle structures you use to squeeze get the full power-training effect from every rep. Give the Super Gripper a go after your next forearm workout, and you'll not only build huge, vascular forearms but develop a bone-crushing grip as well.

Barbell wrist curl—start.

Barbell wrist curl—finish.

Vascularity helps magnify forearm impressiveness.

DON'T OVERUSE WRIST STRAPS

Sometimes bodybuilders use wrist straps for
back exercises, especially pulldowns and deadlifts. They do this so that their grip won't give
out before their back muscles do. While straps
do keep the forearm muscles from being the
weakest link in the chain, overusing them can
hold back forearm development. Gripping
the barbell during deadlifts, for example, can
stimulate forearm growth just as any other
forearm exercise would. Therefore, begin your
back workout without straps. Continue doing
exercises without them until your grip begins
to weaken, then add the straps for grip assis-
tance. That way, you get the maximum forearm stimulation possible during your back
exercises.

The Super Gripper.

Dumbbell wrist curls—start.

Dumbbell wrist curls—finish.

Minimal use of wrist straps combined with the three workouts just discussed will put you well on your way to developing forearms so enormous and defined that everyone will know you're a very serious musclehead, even when you're wearing a loose short-sleeved shirt and baggies. Now, those are forearms.

Intermediate Workout

Seated dumbbell wrist curls	3–4 × 6–10
Reverse curls with wrist flexion	3–4 × 6–10

Advanced Workout

Seated dumbbell wrist curls	4 × 6–10
Reverse curls with wrist flexion	4 × 6–10
Seated barbell wrist curls	4 × 6–10

Larry Scott.

Chapter 9

BUILDING FOREARMS LIKE BOWLING PINS

BY LARRY SCOTT

Sometimes we get so close to a training technique that we don't even think about it. The following phone call reminded me of a wonderful forearm program I'd forgotten about. The call was from a fellow named Emil, and he sounded pretty upset. It went something like this.

"Larry," he said, "there's no way I can use the weight you're telling me to use on forearms."

"I know, Emil. It takes time to build up strength, but be patient. You probably weren't doing forearm work before, were you?"

"Yes, I was, but the weights I was using were less than half of what you're suggesting."

"You're kidding!"

"No, I'm not," he said. "Especially the ones you have me using for the palms-up exercises. They're three times heavier than what I was using!"

"Exactly how are you doing the palms-up exercises?" I asked him. "Are you doing them with your thumbs on the same side of the bar as your fingers?"

"Huh?"

Larry demonstrates proper form.

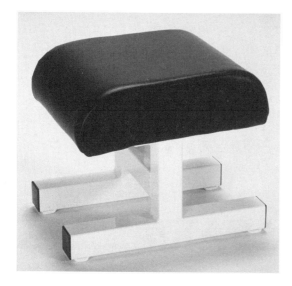

"Are you keeping your fingers and thumbs together rather than wrapping your thumbs around the bar?"

"Yes, I am," he replied. "I already read that in one of your articles. I wouldn't be able to use nearly as much weight if I didn't hold the bar that way."

I continued to try to identify the problem. "What kind of bench are you using?" I asked.

"Oh, just a regular flat bench," Emil replied. "I know you've mentioned that these should be done on a special bench, but I don't have one. I only have the flat bench."

"That explains it," I said. "The normal flat bench just won't do. There's no way you're going to be able to handle a heavy weight using a regular flat bench. You have to be able to get your knees around the bench and your hips lower than your forearms in order to get the weights up.

"When you work forearms on a regular flat bench, you have to hold your forearms way out just to keep the plates from hitting the

Start position: keep your thumbs on the same side of the bar as your fingers for more power.

Finish position.

bench," I continued. "Not only that, but there isn't any way to get the heavy bar into position. That's the reason you can't use much weight. Granted, you can always straddle the bench, with your forearms hanging off the end, but it still limits your strength because your hips are higher than your forearms. When that happens, it's almost impossible to use any body English to help you with the really difficult reps—especially if you're heavy down there and you want to use heavy weights. And you want heavy weights, because they build power even if you're using only partial reps. In fact, the heavy reps you do aren't full reps—they may be only one-quarter or one-eighth reps."

"What!" Emil exclaimed. "You mean I'm not supposed to do full repetitions all the time?"

"Not with the heavy weights. The high poundages are for building tendon strength as well as confidence. The lighter weights are the only ones you do full reps with."

"Oh, no wonder. That explains why you've listed such heavy weights for me. I thought we were supposed to be doing full reps."

"I'm sorry I didn't make that more clear," I said. "I thought I had explained it better. You see, the purpose of working forearms, besides the fact that you want to build giant forearms, is to build power to do heavy biceps curls so that you can have great arms. You can't use heavy weights on curls unless you can get your wrist curled, and that's the big limiter on biceps size. So, you have to build wrist tendons as thick as pencils. That takes some big iron.

"As the weights get heavier and heavier, the movement becomes increasingly less of a

Notice the thumbs' position.

full repetition, in which you let the bar roll all the way down to your fingertips. After that sequence, you finish off the series with 3 to 5 sets of down-the-racks on EZ-curl reverse-grip curls for the back of the forearm. Then you rest a little and repeat the entire series with a 10 percent decrease in weights. Do that two or three times, and it ought to do the trick."

For readers who aren't familiar with my forearm program, here's an excerpt from my book *Loaded Guns* that gives the details:

"Let's assume you have your 12-by-12-inch padded bench, a heavy Olympic bar on one side, and a lighter bar on the other side. You will need both bars because you are going to be supersetting without any rest between heavy and light sets. You will not have time to change weights, so both bars are essential.

"Let's talk about the actual exercise. I suggest 20 repetitions of wrist curls with the heavy bar. I would suggest using only the middle three-fifths of the movement. This one is supposed to be done heavy. Then, without any rest, switch to the other side, and do 20 more repetitions with the light bar. This set should be done with complete repetitions: all the way down to the end of the fingertips and back all the way to the top. After you have done 3 or 4 series of these two exercises, your forearms should have a nice healthy glow, with a fire around the wrist area.

"We then go immediately to reverse curls and do a series of descending-weight reverse-grip curls, using only the middle three-fifths of the exercise. Do 3 or 4 [drop sets]. This will be 1 series. Repeat the series 3 or 4 times.

"This is a great forearm workout, and I can truly say I love it. It's the greatest pump we have in our program, and the gains are unbelievable."

Reverse curls.

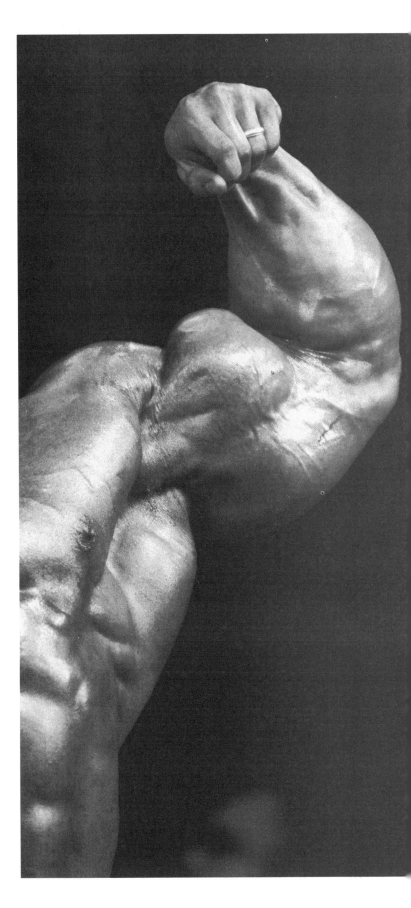

Chapter 10

CAPTAINS OF CRUSH

BY RANDALL J. STROSSEN, PH.D.

The mark of a strongman is his grip, so it's no accident that some of the most memorable stories in strength history involve feats of hand strength. While discussions of grip strength naturally lead to tales of old-timers, there are some modern-day strongmen who bear watching. Let's meet four of them.

One of the most visible of the modern grip men is Gary "the Gripper" Stich, who specializes on the standard grip machine and is the world's best performer in this event. At 5'9½" and about 200 pounds, Gary holds the current right- and left-handed world records on the grip machine, with 310 pounds and 260 pounds, respectively—a far cry from the 50 or so pounds you're likely to see loaded on one of these machines in your local gym. Be forewarned, though, that the grip machine can be a relatively poor test of pure hand strength because a skilled practitioner can essentially perform a seated one-hand shrug that passes for a feat of hand strength.

Even though Gary is best known for his grip-machine world record, he performs another exhibition of grip strength that actu- ally seems more impressive to his fellow grip men: holding an Ironman Super Gripper in front of his chest, he can close it in its toughest position using only his two thumbs. Rumor has it that the Stich household doesn't need a bottle opener.

While he's not strictly a grip man, Steve Sadicaria, a.k.a. "the Mighty Stefan," is a professional strongman in the old-time tradition who must also be counted among those who have unusual strength from the elbow to the fingertips. The compactly built, 5'6", 190-pound Mighty Stefan performs a variety of classic strongman feats in the tradition of Atom and Slim-the-Hammerman. The Mighty Atom originally inspired Steve to be a professional strongman, and Slim-the-Hammerman personally instructed Steve when he was first starting out.

A good number of Sadicaria's feats primarily involve the hands and wrists. For example, bending 60-penny nails and tearing a deck of cards in half are staples in his routine, and his most impressive feat is breaking a piece of No. 8 jack chain in his bare hands.

Reverse wrist curl—start.

Lest you dismiss these accomplishments, however, remember that no one in any of the Mighty Stephan's audiences has been able to perform them.

Another professional strongman who excels in a variety of feats of strength, with an emphasis on hand and wrist power, is 6'1", 250-pound John Brookfield. The mild-mannered Brookfield is a man on whom to consider betting heavily if there were ever a decathlon of hand and wrist strength movements—especially if endurance, as well as pure strength, were a factor. And beyond his impressively versatile skills, John has performed a feat of hand strength that strength historian David P. Willoughby considered to be outright extraordinary: Brookfield can tear a chunk the size of a quarter out of the center of a full deck of cards. Not that this is all John can do with cards: he also tears an entire deck in the box more easily than some people can open their mail, and he has torn two full decks in half at once.

Brookfield got started in the hand-strength area because, while his weight training had allowed him to develop good all-around strength, he felt his grip was lagging. Not only did John set out to correct this situation, but also he was determined to develop the world's strongest grip. That was several years ago. Since then, he has moved relentlessly toward his goal.

John's feats include bending 60-penny nails in half in less than a minute and bending 378 of them in half in less than two hours—both of which are world-record performances. John has also bent two 60-penny nails at once, another bending feat that may well be the best in the world. If the sight of 60-penny nails—six inches long and one-fourth inch in diameter—doesn't impress you, take a look at the l0-by-⅜-inch 100-penny nails John can bend in half anytime. Since he can also bend and break horseshoes at will, you probably won't be surprised to learn that he can wrist-curl more than 300 pounds for reps, even though he doesn't specialize in them. If we had to pick the top all-around performer in feats of hand and wrist strength, John Brookfield would get our nod.

Without a doubt, crushing strength is the most popular and dramatic method for testing grip men. Let's meet the first man named to this elite group, the man who most likely has the strongest grip in the world: Richard Sorin. From going at it in a competitive handshake to comparing performances on a dynamometer, a man's crushing power is usually taken as the measure of his grip, and while Richard Sorin excels in many feats of hand strength, it's his crushing ability that truly puts the 6′5½″, 270-pounder in a class by himself.

For more than 25 years, the standard measure of crushing strength has been the mega-duty hand grippers made by Warren Tetting. The No. 1 stops nearly everyone who tries it, and even men such as Gary Stich and the Mighty Stefan can do only about 10 reps with it. Closing the No. 2 (extra heavy) is in an entirely different league and requires the grip of someone at the level of John Brookfield. And the No. 3 (super)—to the best of our knowledge at the time of this writing—can be closed only by Richard Sorin. Since the average strength athlete will barely budge the No. 3 gripper, it may be easier to appreciate Richard's crushing strength if you know that he can do 34 complete,

Reverse wrist curl—finish.

consecutive repetitions with the No. 2 gripper, which he can also close using just two fingers.

If you are toiling to close the Ironman Super Gripper with its two springs in the tougher position, you may get a kick out of knowing that Richard can do that with two fingers. The other day, he set up an Ironman Super Gripper with four springs in the toughest position and closed it as if it were nothing. As John Brookfield said, "I believe you could search the world over and not find anybody to match Richard's crushing strength." Even so, crushing is not all Richard can do with his hands. He can, in fact, perform a wide range of feats, but let's concentrate on a certain impossible pinch-gripping feat he can do.

The classic mark of an authentic strongman's pinch grip is the ability to pinch-grip two York 35-pound plates together, smooth sides out. Almost nobody can do this, but Richard Sorin first performed the feat when he was a mere 12 years old. Two giant steps more difficult—and a feat that in all likelihood you

will never see anyone do—is the famous pinch grip but with two of the narrow York 45-pound plates that were introduced in 1972.

Yet another two giant steps more difficult is an impossible feat of pinch gripping: hoisting a pair of the old-style (pre-1972) York 45s. Not only are these plates much wider, but also they have very thin rims, so that they must be squeezed together that much harder or they will come crashing down. Richard can do a full deadlift with these old 45s and swing his arm back and forth while pinching them. Now, that's incredible.

Feats of hand strength tie the iron game to its colorful past, and they know little bounds in terms of size, shape, gender, or age of their practitioners. So, start squeezing. Maybe you'll be the next to join the Captains of Crush.

Thomas A. Seward, Ph.D., gives us a firsthand account of helping a trainee develop his forearms using some of the best-proven forearm exercises. Learn how being forewarned can make you forearmed.

Wrist curl—start.

Wrist curl—finish.

Malcolm hadn't been around the gym for more than a year. I heard through the grapevine that he'd joined the Paradise Island Spa, drawn no doubt to the glitter of its chrome-plated dumbbells. He might also have been drawn to the provocative bikini babe who graced the Paradise's ad, offering muscles, fitness, eternal youth, and—if your hormones were active and your imagination overactive—herself. So, it was with some surprise that I found him standing in front of me as I was placing a pair of dumbbells back on the rack after a set of curls.

"Hi, Tom," he said sheepishly. "How you been?"

It was Malcolm, all right, but only the name was the same. Gone were the T-shirt, shorts, and sneakers of a year ago. The new Malcolm was attired in the height of body-building fashion, decked out in fluorescent tights and a "Gorilla Gym" tank top that hung loosely from his shoulders via two gauzelike strands that left all but his navel and lower back bare. His footwear featured magenta laces with mauve tips, and the top of his head was covered with a red bandanna that pulled his long locks back and sent them slithering down his back.

"Malcolm, you look"—I hesitated, not knowing whether to comment on his outfit or his physique, then decided to go for the latter—"great."

"You really think so?"

It was not a rhetorical question. As the only bodybuilder in town who'd ever won a state or regional contest, I was regularly asked to appraise the physiques of the younger athletes.

"I'm going to enter the local contest again," he said. "What do you think my chances are this time?" His request was so filled with optimism and enthusiasm that I gave in and kissed the rest of my workout good-bye.

"OK, Malcolm," I said, resigned to it. "Go put on your posing briefs."

Malcolm rushed into the dressing room and was back in a few short minutes. He began pumping himself up with light dumbbells, and the oil he had hastily slapped on began dripping, splotching the weight-room floor. He was definitely bigger than before, and his definition wasn't half bad.

"All right, Malcolm. Strike some poses for me."

He swung around to face the mirror and grimaced out a double biceps that had his arms quaking with tension. About 10 poses later, I called a halt.

"You can stop now," I told him. "I've seen enough. I say you're good, with signs of greatness."

"Wow, Tom! You're not kidding me, are you?" he asked almost apologetically.

"Of course not. But I said 'signs of greatness,' meaning only that the potential is there."

"Oh," he replied with noticeable irritation.

"To get bigger, you need to pay more attention to the details. You've definitely got some outstanding bodyparts, but I can also see a few weaknesses."

He stared at me blankly.

The incomparable Super Gripper.

"You've trained hard and made real progress," I continued. "That's obvious. Now it's time to stand back and evaluate the results. So, don't be surprised if my words sound a little harsh. It's for your own good."

"OK, Tom. You're right," Malcolm conceded. "I want you to tell me where I need to improve."

"Well," I said, "your most conspicuous weakness is in your forearms."

His jaw dropped, and he was speechless.

"I know what you're thinking: nobody pays any attention to forearms. No one poses them. They're just there, right?"

He shrugged.

"Look at it this way," I said. "Having the rest of your body well developed and in proportion except for your forearms is like having 31 out of 32 teeth in your mouth when you smile."

Malcolm raised his eyebrows.

"All the great bodybuilders of our time, from Grimek through Scott and up to Yates, have known the importance of developing their forearms to the fullest," I continued. "But I dare say you've never done a single forearm exercise in your life."

Now Malcolm began hemming and hawing.

"I'll answer the question for you," I said. "Of course not. And that's why they look so out of place hanging there from those great upper arms of yours. You've got gap-toothed arms."

Malcolm had already resumed his flexing in front of the mirror. He extended one arm after the other, this way and that, manipulating his wrists in an effort to get his forearms to bulge.

"Your forearms would look all right on a guy with smaller upper arms, but right now you have Popeye arms in reverse."

As I made that last comparison, I could see him droop. I was becoming cruel, and it was time to pick up his spirits.

"You've still got a good three months left before the contest," I said. "With some concentrated effort, I believe you can bring your forearms up a bit, maybe even enough to fill in the gap."

"Yeah, that's what I want. But how?"

Forearm strength augments other exercises.

"I thought you'd never ask," I said, laughing to myself. "The first thing you've got to do is add a forearms workout to your routine. Let's go over the exercises first, and then I'll suggest how to fit them into your program."

Malcolm nodded.

"The muscles of the forearm are activated by the flexion of the fingers and the movement of the wrist," I explained. "That's an important point to remember that will help you understand why I suggest specific ways of doing your forearm exercises. The first of these is wrist curls.

"Go ahead and grab a pair of 30-pound dumbbells, and sit on this bench," I instructed. "Put your forearms on your thighs, with your hands extending beyond your knees, palms up. Let your hands hang down, and allow the dumbbells to roll to your fingertips as you open your hands slightly. Now roll the weights back into your palms, grasping them firmly, and curl your wrists upward as far as they'll go. Do about 12 slow, even reps."

Malcolm did exactly as he was told.

"Exchange those 30s for 20s now, and go back to the bench. Place your forearms on your thighs again, but this time hold the dumbbells with your palms facing down. This is called reverse wrist curls. Do about 12 reps."

Malcolm followed my instructions to the letter, and when he finished, he looked up at me in anticipation.

"Now your forearms should be ready for some real work with my pièce de résistance," I said dramatically. I fished my wrist-roller out of my bag and handed it to Malcolm. He looked at it quizzically. It consisted of a 16-inch-long, 1¼-inch-thick wooden dowel with a thin rope wrapped tightly around it. The rope was knotted securely at one end and threaded through a hole I'd drilled in the middle of the dowel.

I took back my work of art, unwound the rope, and attached a 10-pound plate to the other end of the rope. With Malcolm still staring in wonderment, I held the dowel at arm's length with both hands, palms down. Alternating my hands in a wrist action, I rolled the rope onto the dowel, lifting the plate from the floor until it touched the dowel.

"Here," I said, offering him the contraption after I unrolled the rope and lowered the plate back to the floor. "Your turn."

Malcolm took the wrist-roller with the enthusiasm of a child trying out a new toy. He held it out in front of him with his arms parallel to the floor as I had done. The plate rose slowly and steadily as he wound the rope with the brute strength of his forearm muscles. Only after the plate was firmly against the dowel did I speak.

"If you roll your wrists forward and downward to raise the plate, as you just did, you use the underbellies of your forearms. Let the plate back down to the floor now by reversing the action of your wrists."

With some effort, Malcolm followed my instructions again. This time he smiled in relief as the plate touched down.

"Now lift the plate using the same reverse motion you just used to lower it. So, you'll be pulling the backs of your hands toward you, alternating sides, in order to raise the weight," I clarified.

He took a deep breath and completed the task.

"I can feel my forearms starting to burn on top. They're really getting pumped up," he said with relish after he lowered the plate by alternating hands in the forward motion.

"I assume you noticed that each time you rolled the weight up with one hand, you had to loosen your grip somewhat on the other hand so that you could rotate the dowel. That continual relaxing and gripping of your fingers is an added benefit of the wrist roll," I remarked.

"Now it's time to tie your forearms into your biceps workout with front curls." I pointed to an empty Olympic bar on the floor nearby and told him to get it. Then I explained how to perform the movement.

"Hold the bar with your palms down and your hands at a comfortable width," I said. "Now roll your wrists back as far as they'll go, and then curl the bar up toward your

shoulders, keeping your elbows snugly against the sides of your body."

Malcolm began his front curls.

"You'll feel this kind of curl in your lower biceps and the tops of your forearms," I explained. "It creates a continuous tension in both areas so that they're both strongly affected."

He nodded in agreement as he continued to perform rep after strict rep. After about 15 curls, he put the bar down and looked at me with his eyebrows raised high. He was game for more.

"What's next, Tom?"

"That's enough exercises for the moment," I told him. "Get your training journal and a pen, and I'll jot down sets and reps and tell you how to fit them into your arm routine."

He went to his bag and brought out a dog-eared notebook with a pen clipped inside the spiral binding.

"Here's what you should do," I said. "Begin your arm workout with forearms. Attack them full force when you're fresh so you can get the most out of your effort."

Then I wrote the following in the notebook:

Palms-up wrist curls	2 × 12
Palms-down wrist curls	2 × 12
Forward wrist rolls	2 × failure
Backward wrist rolls	2 × failure
Front curls	4 × 12

"After that, you go right into your biceps routine full force," I elaborated. "You'll probably find that your forearms tire before your biceps, but do the best you can with them. Remember, it's your forearms that you need to build up right now, not your biceps."

This time when I spoke strongly, Malcolm didn't bat an eyelash.

"Since you've never really worked your forearms to any extent, I suggest you begin by using a lighter weight than you think you should," I cautioned, "and don't go to failure on the wrist rolls for a couple of weeks either."

"Gotcha! Thanks a lot, Tom." He smiled and shook my hand. Then he gathered up his gear and left the weight room.

A new guy from North Carolina moved into town that year and blew away the competition at the local contest, but the following year belonged to Malcolm. His physique was complete, forearms and all, and he took the Overall and Most Muscular.

Workout 1: Accumulation (Weeks 1 to 3)
Tri-set*

Decline supinated wrist
curls × 60–70 seconds
Decline pronated wrist
curls × 60–70 seconds
Super Gripper × 60–70 seconds

*Perform 3 tri-sets. Take no rest between exercises, and then rest 90 seconds between tri-sets.

Workout 2: Intensification (Weeks 4 to 6)
Superset*

One-arm supinated dumbbell
wrist curls × 30–40 seconds
One-arm pronated dumbbell
wrist curls × 30–40 seconds

Superset*

Super Gripper × 4 reps, squeezing
for 6 seconds
Super Gripper × 10 reps with
continuous tension

*Perform each superset 4 times. Rest 90 seconds between supersets.

Part III

BICEPS TRAINING

Narrow-grip EZ-curl bar.

Chapter 11

EMG ANALYSIS: BICEPS

BY LORENZO CORNACCHIA, TUDOR O. BOMPA, PH.D., BILL McILROY, PH.D., AND LENNY VISCONTI

THE TEST

We tested a number of dumbbell curls. The subjects performed various dumbbell curls while we recorded EMG measurements for the biceps brachii, which enabled us to determine the exercise that produced the greatest amount of electrical activation in the muscle.

Methods

We recruited five healthy volunteer athletes, three men and two women. All the subjects had at least 10 years' experience in strength training and had never used performance-enhancing substances.

We tested them on two separate days. On the first day, we determined their one-rep maxes for the three curl variations. Each athlete performed a warm-up of 4 reps at 50 percent of one-rep max, 3 reps at 80 percent, and 2 reps at 90 percent, with a five-minute rest after each set. The athletes then performed 3 one-rep maxes for each exercise, taking a five-minute rest after each trial.

On the second day, the subjects did 80 percent of one-rep max 5 times, interspersed with three-minute rest intervals.

We tested the following biceps exercises:

1. Standing dumbbell curls performed with an Arm Blaster
2. Seated incline dumbbell curls performed palms up with lateral rotation
3. Seated incline dumbbell curls performed palms up

We measured electromyographic activity during all exercises. All EMG data were rectified and integrated for one second, which is referred to as IEMG. We designated the exercise that yielded the highest IEMG determined at one-rep maximum as IEMG max for the biceps brachii, and we determined IEMG max by computing the average of the three one-rep maxes for each exercise. We expressed IEMG values obtained during 80 percent of one-rep-max sets as a percentage of IEMG max, and we determined IEMG at 80 percent of one-rep maximum by computing the average of the five 80 percent trials.

Wide-grip barbell.

Results and conclusions

Our data indicated that there was no significant in the main exercise effects on the biceps brachii among the three exercises. The IEMG maxes were within 3 percentage points of each other, with the standing dumbbell curls performed with the Arm Blaster at 87 percent, the seated incline dumbbell curls performed palms up with lateral rotation at 86 percent, and the seated incline dumbbell curls performed palms up but without the lateral rotation at 84 percent.

Although the standing curls performed with the Arm Blaster did come out slightly ahead, the results show that all three are effective biceps movements. Note, however, that the experienced bodybuilders who participated in the study used good form on all the movements. For beginners and intermediates, the Arm Blaster is a better choice because it ensures that you maintain strict form.

EMG ANALYSIS: BARBELL CURL VARIATIONS

What type of hand spacing is best: wide or narrow? What type of barbell is best: an Olympic bar or an EZ-curl, or cambered, bar? The age-old bodybuilding answer to those types of questions has always been: The best

Group	Exercise	% IEMG Max	% Difference
5 athletes	1. Standing dumbbell curls with Arm Blaster	87	1 to 2: 1
	2. Seated incline dumbbell curls, palms up with lateral rotation	86	2 to 3: 2
	3. Seated incline dumbbell curls, palms up	84	N/A

Biceps brachii analysis. % IEMG max indicates motor unit activation for the biceps on dumbbell curl variations.

variation is the one that is the most comfortable and that works best for you. That answer, however, never truly gives the people asking the questions a sense of satisfaction. Instead of leaving them eager to try the new idea or plan, it makes them frustrated. For that reason we set out to determine through scientific analysis which hand spacing and barbell type produce the greatest amount of electromyographic activity in the long head of the biceps brachii.

Methods

We recruited four healthy volunteer athletes, two men and two women. All the subjects had at least two years' experience in strength training and had never practiced performance doping.

We tested them on two separate days. On the first day, we determined their one-rep maxes for the four barbell curl variations. Each athlete performed a warm-up of 4 reps at 50 percent of one-rep max, three reps at 80 percent, and 2 reps at 90 percent, with a five-minute rest after each set. The athletes then performed 3 one-rep maxes for each exercise, taking a five-minute rest after each trial.

On the second day, the subjects did 80 percent of one-rep max 5 times, interspersed with three-minute rest intervals.

We tested the following variations of the standing barbell curl:

1. Narrow grip performed with EZ-curl bar
2. Narrow grip performed with Olympic bar
3. Wide grip performed with Olympic bar
4. Wide grip performed with EZ-curl bar

We measured electromyographic activity during all exercises. All EMG data were rectified and integrated for one second, which is referred to as IEMG. We designated the exercise that yielded the highest IEMG determined at one-rep maximum as IEMG max for the biceps brachii, and we determined IEMG max by computing the average of the three one-rep maxes for each exercise. We expressed IEMG values obtained during 80 percent of one-rep-max sets as a percentage of IEMG max, and we determined IEMG at 80 percent of one-rep maximum by computing the average of the five 80 percent trials.

Results

Our data indicated that there was no significant difference in the main exercise effect on the biceps brachii between the narrow-grip standing barbell curl performed with

Group	Exercise	% IEMG Max	% Difference
4 athletes	1. Narrow-grip standing barbell curls on EZ-curl bar	87	1 to 2: 1
	2. Narrow-grip standing barbell curls on Olympic bar	86	2 to 3: 23
	3. Wide-grip standing barbell curls on Olympic bar	63	3 to 4: 2
	4. Wide-grip standing barbell curls on EZ-curl bar	61	N/A

Biceps brachii exercise analysis. % IEMG max indicates motor unit activation.

Incline dumbbell curls.

an EZ-curl bar (87 percent) and the one performed with an Olympic bar (86 percent). There was, however a significant difference between the main exercise effects for the narrow-grip variations and the standing barbell curl performed with a wide grip on the Olympic bar (63 percent) and the EZ-curl bar (61 percent). Therefore, the narrow-grip variations are superior biceps exercises.

Conclusions

Although the percentage of IEMG max for the standing barbell curl performed with a narrow grip on an EZ-curl bar wasn't significantly different from the one for the variation performed with a narrow grip on the Olympic bar, the wide-grip variations showed a considerable drop in EMG activity. Therefore, it's evident that curling with a wide grip doesn't allow you to totally isolate the target muscles and that the shoulder and back muscles play more of a role when you're lifting with a wide grip.

While there was no significant difference between the two narrow-grip variations, the narrow-grip standing barbell curl performed with an EZ-curl bar still produced a 1 percent greater amount of electrical muscular activation in the long head of the biceps brachii, making it the best choice of all.

Although the percentage of IEMG max for the two narrow-grip variations wasn't significantly different, the wide-grip variations showed a considerable drop in EMG activity.

EMG ANALYSIS: DUMBBELL CURL VARIATIONS

Using the incline dumbbell curl, which hand grip—neutral, palms-up, or lateral rotation—is best? The point of these studies is not only to prove scientifically which exercises show the greatest EMG activity in the biceps brachii, but also to answer questions that bodybuilders have been asking for years.

Group	Exercise	% IEMG Max	% Difference
5 athletes	1. Lateral-rotation incline dumbbell curls	88	1 to 2: 1
	2. Palms-up incline dumbbell curls	87	2 to 3: 2
	3. Neutral-grip incline dumbbell curls	85	N/A

Biceps brachii exercise analysis. % IEMG max indicates motor unit activation.

Standing barbell curls with an Arm Blaster.

Methods

We recruited five healthy volunteer athletes, three men and two women. All the subjects had at least two years' experience in strength training and had never practiced performance doping.

We tested them on two separate days. On the first day, we determined their one-rep maxes for three incline dumbbell curl variations. Each athlete performed a warm-up of 4 reps at 50 percent of one-rep max, 3 reps at 80 percent, and 2 reps at 90 percent, with a five-minute rest after each set. The athletes then performed 3 one-rep maxes for each exercise, taking a five-minute rest after each trial.

On the second day, the subjects did 80 percent of one-rep max 5 times, interspersed with three-minute rest intervals.

We tested the following variations of the seated incline dumbbell curl:

1. Lateral-rotation incline dumbbell curl, meaning a palms-up grip in which the hand is rotated outward to where the little finger is higher than the thumb and the forearm is angled away from the torso
2. Palms-up incline dumbbell curl
3. Neutral-grip incline dumbbell curl

We measured electromyographic activity during all exercises. All EMG data were rectified and integrated for one second, which is referred to as IEMG. We designated the exercise that yielded the highest IEMG determined at one-rep maximum as IEMG max for the biceps brachii, and we determined IEMG max by computing the average of the three one-rep maxes for each exercise. We expressed IEMG values obtained during 80 percent of one-rep-max sets as a percentage of IEMG max, and we determined IEMG at 80 percent of one-rep maximum by computing the average of the five 80 percent trials.

Results

Our data indicated that there was no significant difference in the main exercise effect on the biceps brachii among the seated incline dumbbell curl performed with a lateral-rotation grip (88 percent), a palms-up grip (87 percent), and a neutral grip (85 percent). Even so, the lateral-rotation grip did produce slightly more stimulation.

Conclusions

Although the percentage of IEMG max for the seated incline dumbbell curl performed with a lateral-rotation grip wasn't much different from that of the other two variations, the lateral-rotation grip is still the best choice by 1 percent. Nevertheless, the distinctions are

so slight that bodybuilders looking to isolate their biceps brachii should get excellent stimulation no matter which variation of this movement they use.

EMG ANALYSIS: BICEPS

Biceps training is the favorite subject of virtually all bodybuilders. Most professional bodybuilders will tell you that although the biceps is a small muscle group, occupying 35 to 40 percent of the upper arm, it can make or break a physique. Many top bodybuilders claim that a perfect biceps must be thick, round, and full, with a sensational peak. Those criteria seem to hold true, since all the top Olympia winners—such as Lee Haney, Arnold Schwarzenegger, and Lenda Murray—achieved that kind of arm structure.

Here we examine the Arm Blaster, a device that was one of Arnold Schwarzenegger's

Incline curls.

favorites for biceps blasting. Subjects were asked to perform various exercises while we recorded EMG measurements for the biceps brachii.

Methods

We recruited four healthy volunteer athletes, two men and two women. All the subjects had at least two years' experience in strength training and had never used performance-enhancing substances.

We tested them on two separate days. On the first day, we determined their one-rep maxes for the three curl variations. Each athlete performed a warm-up of 4 reps at 50 percent of one-rep max, 3 reps at 80 percent, and 2 reps at 90 percent, with a five-minute rest after each set. The athletes then performed 3 one-rep maxes for each exercise, taking a five-minute rest after each trial.

On the second day, the subjects did 80 percent of one-rep max 5 times, interspersed with three-minute rest intervals.

We tested the following arm exercises:

1. Preacher curls performed with a narrow grip on an Olympic bar
2. Standing barbell curls performed with a narrow grip on an EZ-curl bar and using an Arm Blaster
3. Standing barbell curls performed with a narrow grip on an Olympic bar and using an Arm Blaster

We measured electromyographic activity during all exercises. All EMG data were rectified and integrated for one second, which is referred to as IEMG. We designated the exercise that yielded the highest IEMG determined at one-rep maximum as IEMG max for the biceps brachii, and we determined

Arnold performs curls with an Arm Blaster.

Group	Exercise	% IEMG Max	% Difference
4 athletes	1. Narrow-grip preacher curls with Olympic bar	89	1 to 2: 0
	2. Narrow-grip standing barbell curls with EZ-curl bar and Arm Blaster	89	2 to 3: 1
	3. Narrow-grip standing barbell curls with Olympic bar and Arm Blaster	88	N/A

Biceps brachii analysis. % IEMG max indicates motor unit activation for the biceps on curl variations.

IEMG max by computing the average of the three one-rep maxes for each exercise. We expressed IEMG values obtained during 80 percent of one-rep-max sets as a percentage of IEMG max, and we determined IEMG at 80 percent of one-rep maximum by computing the average of the five 80 percent trials.

Results and conclusions

Our data indicated that there was no significant difference in the main exercise effects on the long head of the biceps brachii among the three exercises. The IEMG max for the narrow-grip preacher curls performed with an Olympic bar and the narrow-grip standing barbell curls performed with an EZ-curl bar and an Arm Blaster came in at 89 percent, while the narrow-grip standing barbell curls performed with an Olympic bar and an Arm Blaster earned 88 percent. Even so, the preacher curls and the EZ-curl bar curls performed with an Arm Blaster did stimulate 1 percent more electrical activity.

The subjects were all experienced bodybuilders, and we made sure that they used strict form on all the exercises. Less seasoned lifters may not get the same results. The beauty of the Arm Blaster is that it helps you maintain strict form throughout the curl's entire range of motion. Therefore, it's advisable for beginning and even intermediate bodybuilders to use this device.

Figure 12.1.

Chapter 12

HAMMER CURLS

BY JOSEPH M. HORRIGAN, D.C.

While the hammer curl is one of the less popular biceps exercises, it has its place in bodybuilding workouts. It also has a purpose for those with wrist, hand, or elbow injuries.

The hammer curl is a two-arm dumbbell curl performed with your palms facing each other. In a basic dumbbell curl, your palms face up, or they rotate from a palms-facing position at the bottom of the movement to a palms-up position at the top. The wrist rotation is called *supination*, and the palms-facing, thumbs-up position is called either *semisupination* or *semipronation*. It goes by both names due to the neutral wrist position when your palms face each other, and that relatively neutral position is precisely what makes the exercise advantageous for some trainees.

Nearly everyone suffers various injuries in life, whether they're training related, work related, sports related, or just due to long-term wear and tear on the joints. Such problems can occur in the wrist as well as in any other joint, and they can make it virtually impossible to perform a standard barbell curl, due to wrist pain.

One relatively common wrist injury is a tear in the triangular fibrocartilage complex (TFCC). If you extend your hand in front of you with your palm down, you can locate the TFCC on the outer region of the wrist, near the bony prominence. As suggested by its name, the TFCC is made of ligaments and a cartilaginous structure. Unusual torque or stress, either chronic or acute, can wear down the cartilage and produce a tear. For example, a trainee who recently came to our office was experiencing significant wrist pain and clicking after he performed curls with a Trap Bar and with his wrists tilted downward. The tilt is called *ulnar deviation*. Performing curls with a Trap Bar and the wrists positioned that way caused a tear in his TFCC. Unfortunately, he required arthroscopic surgery to resolve the injury.

Even more common than TFCC tears are sprains and strains of the wrist. A sprain is an overstretch and/or tear of ligaments that attach bone to bone. A strain is an overstretch and/or tear of tendons that attach muscle to bone. The wrist is made up of eight small

Figure 12.2.

bones known as carpal bones that are positioned in two rows. The eight bones are connected to each other and to the two forearm bones, the ulna and radius, as well as to the five long bones of the hand, the metacarpals.

Tendons and muscles run throughout the wrist and hand, and many combinations of sprains and strains can occur there. Sports that can easily lead to wrist and hand sprains include hockey, football, and the martial arts, particularly jujitsu, which is enjoying peak popularity today thanks to the Grace and Machado families. In addition, healed frac-

tures of forearm and wrist bones can make it difficult to get into the proper position for a barbell curl, due to pain or loss of range of motion.

One of the first variations that trainees make in their workouts is to substitute dumbbells for barbells on certain lifts. Wrist pain can even prevent you from performing the standard dumbbell curl either with your palms up for the entire rep or with your hand rotating from a neutral position to a supinated position.

The hammer curl is so named because you hold the dumbbells the way you would hold a hammer, except that your wrist remains straight throughout the rep. Do not tilt your wrist either upward or downward, which would be *radial deviation* and ulnar deviation, respectively. If you do tilt your wrists down and up during hammer curls, you may injure them, as previously described.

The hammer curl can be a blessing for anyone who suffers from wrist pain and who thought he or she would have to stop doing curls. Even so, the emphasis is different from what you get with a standard dumbbell curl. The standard curl develops the biceps brachii; the brachialis, or lower biceps, which is located underneath the biceps near the elbow; and the brachioradialis, as well as the wrist flexor muscles.

The hammer curl significantly targets the brachioradialis. This muscle, if it's developed, is the large muscle of the forearm. If you extend your forearm out in front of you with your palm down, you can locate the brachioradialis muscle on the top inner area. Its function is to bend, or flex, the elbow and to turn the wrist to a neutral position (palms facing each other) from either a fully pronated (palms-down) or fully supinated (palms-up) position. The brachioradialis is a semisupinator and semipronator in that it performs the first half of both movements but does not complete either. (The brachioradialis is also developed during back exercises such as pullups and rows.)

Hammer curls are usually performed with the dumbbells being curled either simultaneously or alternately. If you curl both dumbbells together, you must be careful not to arch your back too much. That can cause a chronic ache in your lower back, or it can actually cause a lower-back injury, so try to maintain good posture when you do hammer curls. You can help protect your back by keeping your abdominal muscles tight during the exercise.

Demonstrating the movement in the accompanying photos is Frank Vassil, a '97 NABBA Mr. Universe class winner. In Figure 12.1, Frank performs the hammer curl with the dumbbells coming up together, while in Figure 12.2, he uses the alternating-dumbbells style.

If you're an advanced recreational trainee or a competitive bodybuilder and you don't have an injury to the wrist, elbow, or hand that you're working around, hammer curls will add development to your forearms due to their more direct effect on the brachioradialis. Other weight-training athletes have turned to this exercise as well. A few years ago, Superheavyweight World Powerlifting champion Bill Kazmaier, who also won the World's Strongest Man contest several times, used the hammer curl regularly. Kaz was 6'2" and a trim 325 pounds, and he performed lifts of 661 pounds on the bench press with a relatively close grip, 885 pounds on the deadlift, and 920 pounds on the squat. He felt that the brachioradialis development he got from doing hammer curls helped him in the bottom position of the bench press. Many doctors and therapists will argue against that idea, however. We don't know if the brachioradialis development really did help or if Kaz was simply a great bench presser who happened to perform hammer curls. Either way, he had tremendous brachioradialis development and was a very impressive-looking individual.

If you've found that the hammer curl works well in your program, whether or not you have an injury, please don't rush in and add set after set. Anything can be overdone, especially if you aren't used to it. The brachioradialis has a long tendon that goes from the area where the bulk of the muscle stops all the way to the wrist. Overuse of it can produce tendinitis in the area and will require time off from any exercise that produces pain. If you've never performed hammer curls, add just 1 to 2 sets to your workouts for one month. After that, you can add another 1 or 2 sets over the next month if you feel you need them.

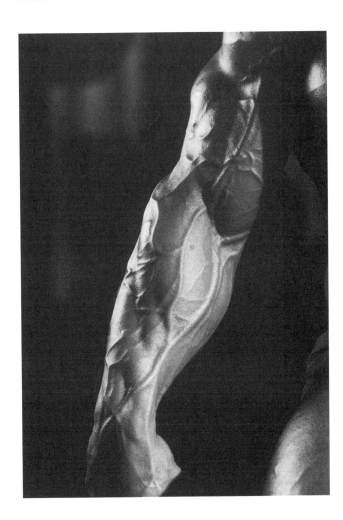

Chapter 13

ARNOLD'S ULTIMATE BICEPS

BY ARNOLD SCHWARZENEGGER AS TOLD TO GENE MOZÉE

I found out many years ago that there is more to peaking the biceps than just curling. It won't do much good to increase the number of sets and the frequency of your biceps work. That approach will likely result in disappointment and overtraining.

If you have been trying for ages without success to improve your biceps peak, my biceps program is just what you need to break through to greater impressiveness and achieve the whole package: size, shape, peak, and cuts. The following routine has worked well for everyone who I've seen use it correctly. All of the guys in the gym at which I trained in Munich before I came to the United States who used my curling techniques developed that egg-shape biceps formation. We called it egg-shape because a superpeaked biceps resembles an egg standing on end.

When I was in Chicago several years ago, I had the occasion to train with my rival, Sergio Oliva. After following Sergio's routine—20 sets of various barbell curls—I grabbed a pair of dumbbells and did 3 sets of alternate dumbbell curls. Sergio asked why I used the

bells after such a heavy biceps routine, and I told him I needed them to fully pump my biceps. Barbell movements build great mass, but you can't work the biceps completely unless you use dumbbells.

The biceps attaches to the shoulder joint and the elbow joint on the forearm. It can do three things: flex the shoulder when raising the arm forward, as when doing a front raise with a dumbbell; flex the elbow, as in a regular curl; and turn the palm face up when the elbow is in the bent position, which is called supination. For building ultimate peak, the rotating, or supinating, aspect of the biceps muscle is the most important. You can do this rotating motion only with dumbbells. No amount of barbell curls ever produced the same intense contraction and resulting soreness that I got from rotating my palms upward and outward as far as I could at the top part of the curling motion.

I am not a big fan of the preacher bench. It's too restricting for my taste. I think it puts too much strain on the elbows as well. Also, I don't think pulley curls build mass and peak

the way dumbbells do, and I could never stand most curling machines, because they are so restrictive.

Bodybuilders generally start a curl with their wrists straight, and as they raise the weight, they bend their wrists toward their shoulders for better leverage. They essentially eliminate gravity and diminish resistance with this technique. Sure, they can handle more weight, but the biceps share the load with the forearms, and the final part of the curl is nullified as far as a peak contraction is concerned. I never curl that way. As I curl, I let my hand lag so that the weight of the dumbbell settles more toward my fingers, and I keep my wrist in this extended position throughout the curling motion. This makes the arm a longer lever—and sustains maximum resistance. Combined with supination, it forms the basis of my biceps peak program.

ARNOLD'S BICEPS EXERCISES

Isolation incline curls

Hold the dumbbells so that your wrists are in the extended position, with your knuckles dropping back toward your forearms. Hold your elbows close to your sides, but keep the dumbbells 8 to 10 inches away from your sides. This focuses the stress on the outer heads of your biceps. Curl the dumbbells as high as possible, with your wrists locked in the extended position. Forcibly tense the biceps at the top of the curl, and continue to force supination of the hands by rotating them until the little finger is higher than the thumb on

each hand. You must feel intense pain with each rep. Do 5 sets of 10 reps with as much weight as you can handle in the strictest form.

Alternate supinating curls

Hold a pair of dumbbells in the standing position, with the backs of your hands facing forward. Curl one dumbbell at a time, and when you start curling, rotate the hand so that the palm faces upward about halfway through the motion. Two inches from the top of the curl, twist your hand so that the little finger is higher than your thumb, and forcibly tense your biceps. The pain of contraction will be incredible. Lower the dumbbell in the exact

Arnold and Franco Columbu.

manner that you curled it, and repeat with the other arm. Do 10 reps with each arm, alternating after each rep. Do 5 sets, with a one-minute rest between sets.

Supinating concentration curls

Almost everyone does this exercise wrong. Try it my way, and watch your biceps take on new bulges. Grasp a dumbbell with your right hand, stand with your feet wide apart, and bend forward until your back is parallel to the floor. Support yourself with your left hand on your left knee. Once again, start with the back of your hand facing forward, and rotate your palm upward as you curl the weight to your deltoid—not your chest. Add the final extra twist and flexion at the top as in the previous exercise. Keep your mind totally focused on the biceps, and try to peak it to the fullest on each rep. After 10 reps, switch to the left hand. Do a total of 5 sets for each arm. Remember, curl to the deltoid on each rep.

TRAINING TIPS

1. Use this program three times a week, with at least one day's rest between biceps workouts.
2. Do all of your biceps exercises together for a maximum flushing and pumping effect. After you finish your biceps work, do triceps and forearms. I like to do all my arm training on the same day that I work my delts—shoulders first, then arms.
3. Concentrate. Focus your full attention on each repetition. Don't look at anything, except your biceps, and don't think of anything, except your biceps. Visualize them getting more peaked and chiseled with each rep.
4. Totally contract the biceps by tensing them during the last two inches on the way up. Lower the weight all the way down to a dead stop on each rep for a full stretch before doing the next rep.
5. Do all peaking exercises moderately slowly so that the biceps feel the tension every inch of the way up and down.
6. Don't cheat. Strict form is essential. Let your biceps do all of the work. Keep forcing the biceps to work harder by increasing the weight whenever possible.
7. Less advanced bodybuilders should do only 3 sets of each movement.

I like total silence when I curl. My mind is inside my biceps. I want no distractions. When I'm doing bench presses, anybody can

make noise, but when I do biceps, I want total quiet so that I can focus every last measure of concentration on forcing my biceps to peak and split to the maximum.

If you want greater peak, deeper separation, and more chiseled cuts, give my program a try. It won't happen overnight. It could take about a year to reshape and peak your biceps, but you'll see good improvement after a couple of months. Everyone who needs biceps improvement can benefit from these training techniques. Use them exactly as I described, and soon you, too, can have more massive, peaked biceps.

Chapter 14

LARRY SCOTT'S CLASSIC BICEPS ROUTINE

BY DAVID PROKOP

Imagine a baseball player today having the opportunity to step back in time to talk to Babe Ruth. Imagine him hearing the Babe say, "All right, kid, I'm gonna tell ya exactly how I hit 60 homers in '27." As a bodybuilder you've got a comparable opportunity here because '60s superstar Larry Scott was to biceps what Babe Ruth was to home runs—the master!

Scott, who won the first two Mr. Olympia contests in 1965 and '66, started bodybuilding about 10 years earlier as a high school student in Pocatello, Idaho. (Although Larry came to prominence in California and, in bodybuilding circles, was considered to be as much a part of that state as the Beach Boys, he was actually born and raised in Idaho.) Oddly enough, what initially got him interested in bodybuilding was a muscle magazine he found at the Pocatello city dump.

"It had a picture on the cover of a bodybuilder named George Pain flexing his triceps," Scott recalled, "and there was an article inside on training triceps. I didn't know anything about exercising, but I saw that picture of George Pain, and I thought, 'Golly, this guy looks incredible!'"

At the time, Larry had reached his full height of 5'8", but he weighed only 120 pounds. Not exactly a Herculean physique. In fact, he weighed less than almost any of the other boys in school. So, he took the magazine home and started doing triceps exercises. Since he didn't have a barbell, he used an old tractor axle instead. He performed mostly barbell kickbacks (although in his case, you'd have to call them axle kickbacks) and supine triceps presses.

"This was between my junior and senior years in high school," Larry related. "I worked only triceps the whole summer. I just wanted to see if I could get any size. I didn't really have a lot of faith that I would grow and that my body would change."

When he returned to school in the fall, Scott started working out at the YMCA and began training his biceps as well, using the following routine:

Beginner Routine*

Standing barbell curls	3 × 10
One-arm dumbbell concentration curls	3 × 10
Zottman dumbbell curls	3 × 10
Total sets: 9	

*This workout was part of a whole-body routine in which Larry would do 1 set of each exercise, then go through the entire sequence 2 more times.

"I didn't know what I was doing," Larry admitted.

"A fellow at the YMCA who was a former boxer gave us advice on how to train. He told us we should go through the whole body 3 times, so we did. What did we know at that age? We went through the whole body, 1 set per exercise, and then we'd do it again and then a third time. It was exhausting, and it was a terrible workout! But that's what I was doing right at first."

The standing barbell curls, one-arm dumbbell concentration curls, and Zottman dumbbell curls were followed by three triceps movements: supine triceps presses with a straight bar, dumbbell kickbacks, and barbell kickbacks. In each case, he did a single set of 8 reps, then moved on to the next exercise. Recalling this primitive training method, Larry said, "What I did for my beginning routine wouldn't be what I would recommend for a beginner now."

Despite the obvious shortcomings of his approach, Scott's progress was such that he placed second in the Best-Built Senior contest at his high school. This wasn't a bodybuilding contest per se, but a loose form of competition in which students cast ballots for the guy they thought had the best physique.

After graduating from high school, Larry moved to Los Angeles to attend an electronics college but returned to Idaho after only six months. While he was in L.A., however, he trained at Bert Goodrich's Gym in Hollywood. Although the gym is long gone, Larry still remembers getting some invaluable training tips there from Lou Degni, a bodybuilder who, he said, "had an incredible physique and was way ahead of his time." It was while he was training in Hollywood, after he had been using the beginner routine for about a year and a half, that Scott formulated the following intermediate regimen:

Intermediate Routine

Standing barbell curls	3 × 6–8
Bent-over dumbbell concentration curls	3 × 6–8
Standing dumbbell curls	3 × 6–8
Total sets: 9	

By this time, Larry had switched to doing 3 sets of each exercise, gradually increasing the weight with each set, before moving on to the next bodypart. That's the approach he was following when he returned to Idaho—until the day the legendary Steve Reeves visited the gym where Scott and his bodybuilding buddies were training.

"We found that training the whole body in each workout while trying to increase the weight with each set wasn't very effective,"

Larry related, "so we asked Steve what he thought about what we were doing.

"'That's crazy!' he said. 'You should change your way of training and start using a down-the-rack training system.' He didn't tell us which exercises to do, but he told us how to do them. He said, 'Do a set with 100 pounds, decrease the weight, and do a set with 90 pounds; decrease it again, and do it with 80 pounds. . . .' And so, we started training in a down-the-rack fashion, but we still continued to train the entire body each workout."

During this intermediate phase of his training, Scott was doing 9 sets for biceps and 9 for triceps at each workout. The triceps exercises were barbell kickbacks, one-arm dumbbell kickbacks, and the supine triceps presses. Although he was no longer going from exercise to exercise with every set, he was still training his entire body at each workout. Remember, however, that this was the late '50s,

and the split system of training we take for granted now hadn't yet been introduced.

"We didn't know anything about a split routine," Larry said. "By the way, that came out of Salt Lake City from a fellow by the name of Dave Fitzen, who split the body in half, training half the body one day, the other half the next day. That occurred right around 1960. A lot of people take credit for that, but he was the one who came out with that 'split' concept. And a number of us from Idaho and Utah brought it out to California. It was quite a novel way to train the muscles more intensely and give them time to recuperate. It was a new concept. Nobody had ever thought of that before. We had always trained the whole body in one day, and it was exhausting!"

After about a year and a half on this intermediate routine, during which time Scott still emphasized triceps training much more than biceps work ("I'd go through the biceps training, but I'd really put my everything into the triceps"), he won the Mr. Idaho title. Larry now weighed about 155 pounds, and his arms measured about 15¼ inches. Then he moved to Los Angeles and started the meteoric buildup that resulted in his becoming the greatest bodybuilder in the world—and produced those beautifully peaked, 20-plus-inch arms that connoisseurs of the sport talk about to this day.

Despite the heavy emphasis on triceps training in his beginner and intermediate days, Scott was to learn something rather ironic when he returned to Los Angeles—specifically, that his biceps were the more impressive bodypart!

"I happened to go into a club in North Hollywood, and there was a fellow in there by the name of Reid Flippen," he explained. "He was from Utah, and I was from Idaho, so we had a little bit in common, I guess. And he said, 'Your arms look pretty good; let me see them.' So, I flexed my triceps. He said, 'Your triceps isn't your best part; it's your biceps.' So, I thought, 'Oh, no!,' thinking of the attention I had focused on the triceps. Up to that point, I had never even liked biceps work. But I guess the genetic shape was what he was referring to. And so, then I started working more on biceps."

Every serious student of bodybuilding history knows, of course, that during his heydey Larry Scott trained at Vince's Gym in Studio City, which is in the San Fernando Valley, and that he became so identified with arm development and training that two new terms were added to the lexicon of the sport: "Scott curls" (which are actually preacher curls) and the "Scott bench" (which, again, is a preacher bench, albeit of rather unique design).

The following is the arm routine that enabled Larry Scott to go from 15¼- to almost 21-inch arms in just a few years—and earned him an honored spot among the all-time greats of the sport:

Advanced Routine
Dumbbell curls on preacher bench
   6 reps, 4 burns
Wide-grip preacher bench barbell curls
   6 reps, 4 burns
Reverse-grip curls with EZ-curl bar
   6 reps, 4 burns
Series repeated 5 times.
Total sets: 15

"I was introduced to the preacher bench by Vince [Gironda]," Larry continued. "I really worked hard on the preacher bench, taking advantage of the low connection I had on the

biceps. So, I got really involved in that, and my arms really started to grow.

"For one thing, my training was much better. Vince had a lot of unique, well-designed equipment. I started to make good progress."

"Good progress" is the understatement of the century. After Larry had been training at Vince's Gym for about a year, he placed third in the Mr. Los Angeles contest—a significant step up for him, considering the higher quality of competition he faced in California. (Remember, only a year earlier, he had weighed 155 pounds at a height of 5′8″.) And that was just the beginning.

"About two months after the L.A. contest, I met Rheo Blair, a nutritionist. I started taking his protein powder—the first time I'd taken protein—and I put on 8 pounds in just two months, which was unheard of for me. It was just really incredible! That protein must have been exactly what my body needed.

"I put on 8 pounds of muscle! I mean, 8 pounds would have normally taken me about two years. To put it on in two months was just amazing!

"A year later, I won the Mr. California, which was a total surprise to me and to everyone else," he continued. "So, I was really excited about my training and my progress. I kept training harder and harder, but my biceps routine stayed pretty much the same. Just the intensity changed.

"I was doing a set of dumbbell curls on the preacher bench. Then, with no rest, I would do a set of barbell wide-grip curls on the bench and then a set of reverse-grip EZ-bar curls—again, with no rest. I would do 5 series of these three exercises, resting only long enough between series so my training partner could do his.

"So, I was doing 5 series of 3 sets, and on each exercise I would do 6 repetitions with 4 burns at the end of each set. Burns, of course, are small, quarter movements either at the top or the bottom of the exercise. I'd do them at the top until I got a little bored with it, and then I'd do them at the bottom.

"That routine really got my arms to grow. That was a very effective program. As a matter of fact, to this day I've not found anything that effective for building biceps."

Were the burns the key to this routine? Was that the magic that was at work, or was it something else? "Well, I think the thing that worked so well was, first, I had—genetically—a low connection on the biceps. And the preacher bench works low biceps. And then there was the intensity of this type of workout—it's extremely painful! That series I just

mentioned is very, very painful, but it just blows the arms up like nothing else I've ever seen—if the preacher bench is designed correctly.

"Most of the benches you see have a flat face, and they don't work. People who hear me talk about arm training go out and try that on a regular preacher bench, and they say, 'Ah, he must have been a genetic freak, because that doesn't work for me at all.' That's because they have a lousy bench.

"As a matter of fact, I remember Arnold saying to me, 'I don't know how you ever made any progress on a preacher bench.' And I went in to shoot some photos on the preacher bench at the gym in Venice where he was training, and I thought, 'God, no wonder he says that. This is terrible!'

"The correct design of the bench is that it has to have a face that's convex rather than flat. In other words, the face should bulge out in the middle. Most preacher benches are flat because they're easier to manufacture that way. But the bench has to have a convex face. And the area at the top where you place your armpits has to be rounded and well padded, because you're going to be bearing down real hard on that bench when you're doing the curls. Most benches have a sharp ridge on top, and it hurts your armpits.

"Most preacher benches are also designed with the post set back, and when the exercise really gets difficult, you hit that post with your groin, so you can't really get into it hard. The post should be offset toward the front. Manufacturers also make the face of the preacher bench too long, so the dumbbells hit the face of the bench at the bottom. What you want is a bench that has a short face, bulging out in the middle and rounded on both sides, and also rounded and padded where your armpits are, with the post placed toward the front so your groin won't be pressing up against it. If you get all those little features on it, it's a great piece of equipment!"

In fact, Scott said that the design of the bench is so important that nowadays when he's on the road and does biceps work on a regular, flat-faced preacher bench, he loses

arm size! "Then when I get back on the right equipment again, my arms come back up. So, the normal preacher benches that you see won't give you the results that you want. I mean, you can make better progress doing incline dumbbell curls than you can doing curls on the normal preacher bench, but you get a good preacher bench and, boy, you can build some arms!"

With single-minded determination, going through a 4-pound tin of protein powder every eight days and drinking some two and a half gallons of milk a day, Larry actually built up to a peak bodyweight of 212 pounds in '65 and '66. His best competitive weight when he was Mr. Olympia was about 205. As for those arms, he said, "My arms got so big that they were hard to carry around. My traps just got exhausted carrying them. I used to tuck my thumbs into my belt loops just to give my traps a rest."

It's significant that all during those glory days of the '60s, Larry Scott's biceps routine remained the same—right down to the order of the exercises and even how he did each exercise. The routine was like a magic formula he had discovered, and he wasn't about to tamper with it.

"I had a particular style for each of the different curls," he explained. "The dumbbell curls were done 'loose' style: I didn't care how I got 'em up; I just wanted to get them up anyway I could. Then the barbell curls were done very strict. I would get my armpits way down on the bench, and I would make sure that my form was totally strict. As a matter of fact, the magic to that whole combination is the barbell curl. You do the exercise totally strict, your body over the bench; you don't help the arms at all with even a little bit of lean-back, and that's what really gives you the tremendous growth.

"Then you finish off, when your arms are just about to die, with reverse-grip EZ-bar curls, and that works the brachioradialis and hits the low biceps. The biceps is exhausted at that point, but the brachioradialis isn't."

And it's also a curling muscle, so you can use that muscle to help you put extra work into the low biceps. It really gives you a great pump. In other words, the pattern to this routine was to do the dumbbell curls with as much weight as possible to basically tire the biceps, then place maximum concentrated stress on the biceps by doing the barbell curls in a very strict fashion and, finally, when the arms were all but dead, do still another exercise that worked a part of the biceps—the brachioradialis—that still had some life left. Clearly, it's a routine that reflects a touch of genius.

"And it never worked as well if I split those exercises up or changed the order of the exercises," Scott said. "That combination had a magic quality to it."

During this advanced phase of his training, Larry worked biceps twice a week, following, of course, a split routine. He always trained arms, shoulders, and neck together. In his beginner days, he trained his arms three times a week, and during the intermediate phase, he worked them four times a week.

"By the way," he continued, "that bench that Vince had, we've improved it in several respects; so, it's an even better piece of equipment now. You know, after doing curls on that thing for 20 years or more as I've done, you've got to be pretty dumb not to figure out some ways to make it better."

Looking back over the evolution of his biceps training, Larry said he wouldn't change a thing about his advanced routine. The beginning and intermediate routines are quite another matter, however.

"They were terrible," Scott admitted. "I would never recommend that anyone use those. I would recommend that a beginner or an intermediate do it totally differently. A beginner doesn't know yet what is right or wrong, so he has to just have blind faith as he's trying different exercises. I'd suggest he change exercises at least every week, because the changing stress provides much better growth, and it rejuvenates the ligaments and tendons, so you don't get into injury all the time.

"I'd make sure I did only 6 repetitions; 6 is a better figure for growth than 8 or 10. I would also do the burns; I think the burns are wonderful to add some extra stress to it. I would do probably no more than 9 sets per bodypart, increasing the intensity. I would also vary the way I trained. Instead of doing just down-the-rack workouts, I'd do down-the-rack; I'd do straight sets; I'd do supersets. I'd change that system of training a lot. I wouldn't do the same thing over and over again. And, of course, I'd follow a split routine rather than training the whole body in each workout, as I was doing."

Larry made one final point about biceps training, and it's important to anyone who wants to build Mr. Olympia–quality arms. "When I got to the advanced stage of my training in the '60s," he said, "I began to realize that I couldn't go up to the heavier weights unless I began to work and strengthen my forearms. And so, I started to train the forearms really hard so that I could get the wrist curled at the bottom of the movement on the preacher bench. When you're doing biceps curls and you're way down on the bench, you can't get the bar up unless you get your wrists curled, and you can't get the wrists curled unless you have the forearm strength. So, I started working forearms very hard, and I noted that as I worked forearms harder, I could use heavier weights in the biceps exercises. Consequently, it was the forearms that were the key to building bigger biceps."

Chapter 15

BASEBALL BICEPS

BY DAVE TUTTLE

There's no question that biceps development is high on most bodybuilders' priority list. That may seem strange, since the biceps is clearly one of the smaller muscle groups. Even with the most gargantuan development, its size pales in comparison with the quadriceps or back. Yet, whatever logic may dictate, bodybuilders are emotionally drawn to the king of bodyparts: the biceps.

Trainees hope to achieve two main goals with this muscle group: maximum circumference and the highest peak. The two don't necessarily go hand in hand. The biceps area could be thick and relatively flat, or it could be thin, yet soar upward in a towering peak.

THE FUNCTION OF THE BICEPS MUSCLES

The area commonly known as the biceps is technically referred to as the *anterior humeral region*, and it includes the coraco-brachialis, the biceps brachii, and the brachialis anticus. The *coraco-brachialis* is the smallest of the three,

and it's located in the upper and inner part of the arm. It originates at a bony area near the collarbone known as the coracoid process and inserts onto the middle of the humerus, or upper-arm bone, by means of a flat tendon. The coraco-brachialis permits adduction of the arm, which is the action of bringing it toward the trunk. It also helps elevate the arm toward the scapula, the shoulder blade.

Flex Wheeler.

The *biceps brachii* is by far the largest muscle in the region. It has two origins, which is why we say *biceps* instead of *bicep*. The short head originates at the coracoid process, where it is fused with the coraco-brachialis, while the long head originates from the upper portion of the glenoid cavity, an oval depression into which the head of the humerus bone fits. The two heads join about halfway down the humerus. The biceps inserts below the elbow on the radius, which is the smaller of the forearm bones.

This muscle flexes the elbow and supinates, or rotates, the radius. You can observe this

supination by placing your forearm at a 90-degree angle to the upper arm and turning your hand from palm-down to palm-up.

The *brachialis anticus* is a broad muscle that covers the elbow joint and the lower half of the front of the humerus. It originates on the humerus and inserts on the front surface of the ulna, which is the larger forearm bone. It is a major flexor of the elbow and protects the elbow joint as well.

THREE-LEVEL PROGRAM

Always start with a warm-up on every exercise, using 40 percent of the weight you'll lift on your 3 main sets. This is important because each exercise works the muscles differently. Try to do at least 6 reps per set, and focus on progressive resistance. When you can do 10 reps with a given weight, increase the weight. This will temporarily lower the number of reps you can do, but over time you'll gain strength and work up to 10 reps again. Keep repeating this process, and watch as your biceps muscles balloon in size and shape.

NOVICE WORKOUT

Since the three muscles described are recruited to some extent every time you train chest, back, or shoulders, it's easy to overtrain the biceps. In fact, overtraining may be as much of a factor in holding back your growth as improper exercise technique. To ensure that you don't overtrain, the novice workout includes only one exercise. This will allow you to use maximum intensity in executing the movement.

Dumbbell curls   3 × 6–10

Dumbbell curls

You can perform this exercise either seated on a bench or standing up. In both cases, however, only your arms should move. You must

Dumbbell curls.

Barbell preacher curls.

keep the rest of your body stationary. The goal here is to isolate the biceps muscles. If you swing your body, you defeat the purpose.

Take a dumbbell in each hand, and hold them at your sides, with your palms facing your legs. Now rotate one of your palms so that it faces forward, and begin the movement. Bring the weight up until the biceps is completely contracted and the dumbbell is almost touching your shoulder. Keep your upper arm next to your side. Twist the dumbbell at the top so that your little finger is forced closest to the shoulder. This provides the fullest contraction. Lower the arm to the starting position, and do the same movement with your other arm. Continue alternating arms until you complete the required reps.

If you find that you're stronger in one arm than the other, start with the weaker arm. Continue to alternate your arms as indicated, forcing out repetitions until you can't get any more with the weaker arm, then stop—even if you could do more with your stronger arm. In time, this should reduce the strength differential.

INTERMEDIATE WORKOUT

The intermediate workout includes a second exercise for added development.

Dumbbell curls	3–4 × 6–10
Preacher curls	3–4 × 6–10

Preacher curls

If you use it properly, the preacher bench eliminates all cheating from the curling movement. Therefore, you probably won't be able to

Jonathan Lawson.

lift as much weight as you can on biceps exercises that permit swinging.

Select a relatively light dumbbell. (If you're not sure how much you can lift, err on the side of caution for your first set.) Place your arm firmly on the portion of the preacher bench that's at a 45-degree angle to the floor. Put a dumbbell in the hand of your weaker arm. Position your upper arm so that the biceps brachii and your palm are facing directly upward.

Without moving your trunk or shoulders, slowly lift the dumbbell until your forearm touches your biceps. Crunch your forearm against the biceps, and pull the dumbbell as close to your shoulder as you can without bending your wrist. This will give your biceps brachii and brachialis anticus a great workout. (Since the arm is stationary on the preacher bench, the coraco-brachialis isn't called into play.) Slowly lower the weight to its original position, and repeat.

Once you've performed as many repetitions as you can with your weaker arm, repeat the exercise with your stronger arm. Stop after you do the same number of repetitions you did with your weaker arm.

ADVANCED WORKOUT

The elite routine piles on the intensity with a third exercise.

Dumbbell curls	4 × 6–10
Preacher curls	4 × 6–10
Standing EZ-curl bar curls	4 × 6–10

Standing EZ-curl bar curls

An EZ-curl bar is a cambered barbell that has a Z shape. Place the EZ-curl bar in front of you. Position your feet at approximately shoulder width. Let your arms hang naturally at your sides, then rotate them slightly so that your thumbs point directly ahead. This will put your palms at an approximate 45-degree angle to your legs.

Squat, and place your hands on the two parts of the bar that most closely match the positioning of your hands. Grip the bar, and stand up. Without swinging your body or moving your shoulders, lift the bar until your forearms are as close to your biceps as possible. Your upper arms should remain close to your sides. Crunch your biceps. Then lower the bar to the starting position, and repeat.

Roland Kickinger.

Sometimes bodybuilders try to raise the cambered bar even farther so that their upper arms are parallel to the ground at the end of the movement. The last part of the motion recruits the shoulders, however, not the biceps. Once your forearm is next to your upper arm, the biceps has contracted as much as it can. Train your shoulders on shoulder day.

BICEPS PEAKS AND GENETICS

There's a great deal of misunderstanding about the role of genetics in the development of a great biceps peak. Sometimes athletes are told that they can train the "middle" of the biceps brachii in order to increase its peak. Alas, there's no truth to this rumor. The physical relationship between your biceps brachii's length and its height is determined genetically and cannot be altered. No exercise will enable you to get a greater peak per se, but the greater the volume of all three of your biceps muscles, the higher your peak will be when you contract them.

The best course of action is to train your biceps muscles properly with full intensity and sufficient recuperation. Avoid overtraining, and allow your guns to grow to their full genetic potential. Here's another tip: When you flex your arms during competition, make sure that you leave a space between your biceps and forearm. When the judges see your biceps peak next to the depth of your elbow joint, it will seem even higher. It may be an optical illusion, but who cares?

So, blast your guns into massive proportions, and show them off correctly. Those baseball-size biceps you've dreamed about can be yours!

Chapter 16

HEAVILY ARMED AT HOME: BICEPS

BY STEVE HOLMAN

If your arms aren't stretching your shirtsleeves and causing people to do double takes when you wear a T-shirt, perhaps it's time you quit babying them. With some precise, intense bi-tri specialization, you can turn your derringers into cannons, and you can do it in your own home gym as long as you're willing to turn up the intensity. Don't come back with that old excuse that your arms would be huge if only you had access to all the great machines at a commercial gym. To tell you the truth, barbells and dumbbells are the best arm-building tools around. You just have to use them correctly—as in doing the right exercises in the proper order with the correct form.

Each of your upper-arm muscles has a range of motion that you should train for fast, full development. For example, your biceps are fully contracted when your upper arm is up next to your head and your elbow is bent down, with your little finger twisting outward. Your biceps are fully stretched when your arm is straight, down, and back behind your torso. Between those two extreme positions, there's a middle range, where your upper arms are slightly in front of your torso as you curl. If you move your arm from beside your head to past your torso as you straighten it, you put the biceps through its full range of motion. Of course, no single exercise hits this entire range, so we use three exercises to train the biceps at three points along the arc.

You may recognize this as a description of Positions-of-Flexion training, which is explained in the book *Critical Mass* (published by *Ironman*). Rather than recommend a standard POF arm routine, however, I suggest you try something a little more radical. It's somewhat more dangerous than standard POF protocol because you do the stretch-position exercise first—but you do it for a very specific reason.

Because of the muscle-fiber-activation capabilities of the myotatic, or stretch, reflex, incline dumbbell curls prime your biceps for ultimate stimulation. By twitching out of the bottom of each rep, you send an emergency-response signal to your nervous system and

curls. You can use slightly less-than-strict form so that you get some synergy, or muscle teamwork, from your front delts, but don't turn the movement into reverse power cleans. Give the bar a little heave—enough to get it moving in order to overload the biceps, but not enough to herniate a disk in your lower back.

After the 2 sets of barbell curls, your bi's will be swollen to the bursting point, but there's still one more exercise to go. To finish off those peaks, do 1 set of nonsupport concentration curls with a squeeze at the top of each rep. This exercise gets your biceps close to complete contraction—where your upper arm

get an inordinate number of fibers to fire. Do this first, and you set the stage for some tremendous stimulation for the exercises to follow.

After 2 sets of 8 to 10 reps of this fiber jolter, move to barbell curls. This will hit the belly of the biceps with a pump and ache that you won't believe, especially after the fiber recruitment you achieved with the incline is next to your head—so, try to stay bent over to at least parallel throughout the set. If you really feel you need it, you can add a second set, but most bodybuilders' biceps will be completely blown out after the 5 sets. Here's your home-gym biceps specialization blast:

Incline curls	2 × 8–10*
Barbell curls	2 × 8–10
Nonsupported concentration curls	1–2 × 8–10

*Do 2 progressively heavier warm-up sets to prevent injury. Remember, this is a stretch-position movement, and, because you're doing it first, it could cause a muscle tear if you don't warm up properly.

Part IV

TRICEPS TRAINING

Chapter 17

EMG ANALYSIS: TRICEPS

BY LORENZO CORNACCHIA, TUDOR O. BOMPA, PH.D., AND LENNY VISCONTI

Pro bodybuilders don't usually win major titles if they don't have great arm development. The triceps muscle consists of three heads that originate at various points in the shoulder: the long head on the scapula, the lateral head on the back of the humerus (upper-arm bone) in front of the radial groove, and the medial head on the back of the humerus behind the radial groove. The heads insert via a large bandlike tendon over the ulna (larger lower-arm bone) and fascia of the forearm at the elbow. The primary function of the triceps is to extend the forearm at the elbow joint.

One of the most commonly used exercises for triceps training is the pushdown, also known as the pressdown, and it's performed on a high cable with any number of different bar attachments. Which is the most effective variation? We set out to determine just that through scientific analysis. This was a three-part experiment.

PART 1

In Part 1, we focused on the lateral, or outer, head of the triceps.

Methods

We recruited four healthy volunteer athletes, two men and two women. All the subjects had at least two years' experience in strength training and had never practiced performance doping.

We tested them on two separate days. On the first day, we determined their one-rep maxes for the four pushdown variations. Each athlete performed a warm-up of 4 reps at 50 percent of one-rep max, 3 reps at 80 percent, and 2 reps at 90 percent, with a five-minute rest after each set. The athletes then performed 3 one-rep maxes for each exercise, taking a five-minute rest after each trial.

2. Angled-bar pushdowns
3. Lat-bar pushdowns
4. Straight-bar pushdowns

We measured electromyographic activity during all exercises. All EMG data were rectified and integrated for one second, which is referred to as IEMG. We designated the exercise that yielded the highest IEMG determined at one-rep maximum as IEMG max for the outer head of the triceps, and we determined IEMG max by computing the average of the three one-rep maxes for each exercise. We expressed IEMG values obtained during 80 percent of one-rep-max sets as a percentage of IEMG max, and we determined IEMG at 80 percent of one-rep maximum by computing the average of the five 80 percent trials.

Results and conclusions

Our data indicated that there was a significant difference in the main exercise effect on the outer head of the triceps brachii between the angled-bar pushdowns performed with rotation (90 percent) and those for the angled-bar (85 percent), lat-bar (84 percent), and straight-bar (83 percent) variations. Therefore, pushdowns performed on an angled bar with rotation are the best choice for working the outer head, and you should include them in your triceps program whenever possible.

On the second day, the subjects did 80 percent of one-rep max 5 times, interspersed with three-minute rest intervals.

We tested the following variations of the pushdown:

1. Angled-bar pushdowns with rotation—a rotating sleeve on the bar

Group	Exercise	% IEMG Max	% Difference
4 athletes	1. Angled-bar pushdowns with rotation—a rotating sleeve on the bar	90	1 to 2: 5
	2. Angled-bar pushdowns	85	2 to 3: 1
	3. Lat-bar pushdowns	84	3 to 4: 1
	4. Straight-bar pushdowns	83	N/A

Triceps brachii exercise analysis. % IEMG max indicates motor unit activation for the lateral head.

PART 2

Next we looked at triceps pressing movements to determine if exercises such as the close-grip bench press or pullover and press are good mass builders for the outer head.

Methods

We recruited four healthy volunteer athletes, two men and two women. All the subjects had at least two years' experience in strength training and had never practiced performance doping.

We tested them on two separate days. On the first day, we determined their one-rep maxes for the four pressing variations. Each athlete performed a warm-up of 4 reps at 50 percent of one-rep max, 3 reps at 80 percent, and 2 reps at 90 percent, with a five-minute rest after each set. The athletes then performed 3 one-rep maxes for each exercise, taking a five-minute rest after each trial.

On the second day, the subjects did 80 percent of one-rep max 5 times, interspersed with three-minute rest intervals.

We tested the following pressing exercises for the triceps:

1. Reverse narrow-grip bench presses
2. Pullover and presses
3. EZ-curl bar close-grip bench presses
4. Olympic bar close-grip bench presses

We measured electromyographic activity during all exercises. All EMG data were rectified and integrated for one second, which is referred to as IEMG. We designated the exercise that yielded the highest IEMG determined at one-rep maximum as IEMG max for the triceps brachii, and we determined IEMG max by computing the average of the three one-rep maxes for each exercise. We expressed IEMG values obtained during 80 percent of one-rep-max sets as a percentage of IEMG max, and we determined IEMG at 80 percent of one-rep maximum by computing the average of the five 80 percent trials.

Results and conclusions

Our data (see table on page 146) indicated that there was no significant difference in the main exercise effect on the outer head of the triceps between reverse narrow-grip bench presses (89 percent) and pullover and presses (87 percent); however, there was a significant difference in the main effect for the reverse narrow-grip benches and the close-grip benches performed with an EZ-curl bar (82 percent) and those performed with an Olympic bar (76 percent). Therefore, reverse bench presses performed with a narrow grip produce the most electrical activation for the triceps brachii, and if you're looking to include a pressing movement in your triceps routine, that's the best one to choose.

PART 3

In Part 3 we set out to discover through scientific analysis which overhead dumbbell triceps exercise gets the nod. Subjects were asked to

1. Lateral, 2. long, 3. medial.

Close-grip bench with Olympic bar.

tions. Each athlete performed a warm-up of 4 reps at 50 percent of one-rep max, 3 reps at 80 percent, and 2 reps at 90 percent, with a five-minute rest after each set. The athletes then performed 3 one-rep maxes for each exercise, taking a five-minute rest after each trial.

On the second day, the subjects did 80 percent of one-rep max 5 times, interspersed with three-minute rest intervals.

We tested the following overhead exercises for the triceps:

1. Neutral-grip dumbbell triceps extensions
2. Dumbbell triceps extensions with rotation
3. Reverse-grip dumbbell triceps extensions

We measured electromyographic activity during all exercises. All EMG data were rectified and integrated for one second, which is referred to as IEMG. We designated the exercise that yielded the highest IEMG determined at one-rep maximum as IEMG max for the triceps brachii, and we determined IEMG max by computing the average of the three one-rep maxes for each exercise. We expressed IEMG values obtained during 80 percent of one-rep-max sets as a percentage of IEMG max, and we determined IEMG at 80 percent of one-rep maximum by computing the average of the five 80 percent trials.

perform three variations using different grips and rotations.

Methods

We recruited four healthy volunteer athletes, two men and two women. All the subjects had at least two years' experience in strength training and had never practiced performance doping.

We tested them on two separate days. On the first day, we determined their one-rep maxes for the three triceps extension varia-

Group	Exercise	% IEMG Max	% Difference
4 athletes	1. Reverse narrow-grip bench presses	89	1 to 2: 2
	2. Pullover and presses	87	2 to 3: 5
	3. EZ-curl bar close-grip bench presses	82	3 to 4: 6
	4. Olympic bar close-grip bench presses	76	N/A

Triceps brachii exercise analysis. % IEMG max indicates motor unit activation for the lateral head.

Group	Exercise	% IEMG Max	% Difference
4 athletes	1. Neutral-grip dumbbell triceps extensions	80	1 to 2: 2
	2. Dumbbell triceps extensions with rotation	78	2 to 3: 1
	3. Reverse-grip dumbbell triceps extensions	77	N/A

Triceps brachii exercise analysis. % IEMG max indicates motor unit activation for the lateral head.

Results and conclusions

Our data indicated that there was no significant difference in the main exercise effect on the outer head of the triceps among the neutral-grip dumbbell triceps extension (80 percent) and those for the variation performed with rotation (78 percent) and the variation performed with a reverse grip (77 percent). Nevertheless, the results of the study indicate that the neutral grip produces the greatest amount of electrical activation for the lateral head of the triceps. Therefore, if you're looking to add another triceps exercise to your workout, the overhead dumbbell extension performed with a neutral grip would be an excellent choice.

Dumbbell triceps extensions are a great triceps builder.   Romeo Villarino.

Figure 18.1.

Chapter 18

STANDING TRICEPS EXTENSIONS

BY JOSEPH M. HORRIGAN, D.C.

Arm strength has been valued for eons. In fact, there's an ancient Nordic expression that a person would "give his strong right arm" for some desired outcome or event.

Arm-training articles frequently point out that the triceps is the largest arm muscle and that you should make sure it receives its share of work. The triceps brachii is made up of three heads, or muscle bellies: the lateral, medial, and long heads. The lateral head is located on the outer arm, and, when it's developed and your body fat is low enough to make it stand out, it's what's known as a "good cut." The lateral head originates, or attaches, on the upper third of the upper-arm bone, the humerus. The medial head is located on the inner side of the arm and originates on the lower part of the humerus. When the medial head is developed, the triceps looks thick near the elbow.

The long head is the most interesting and the most important for upper-arm bulk. It is the inner portion of the arm, and it accounts for the bulk of the triceps. The long head originates on the shoulder blade, or scapula,

below the glenoid fossa, the socket joint of the shoulder.

The function of the lateral and medial heads is to extend, or straighten, the elbow. Some studies have indicated that the last part of extension relies significantly on the medial head.

The long head is considered a two-joint muscle because it passes over the elbow and shoulder. While it does extend the elbow, it also extends the shoulder. Shoulder extension is a movement that pulls your arm down toward your side if it's raised in front of you, as in a front deltoid raise. That's important because a two-joint muscle must be stretched at both joints to be fully facilitated, or recruited.

The lateral and medial heads receive a tremendous amount of work in chest and shoulder training. The bench press, incline press, military press, behind-the-neck press, and dip cause the triceps to perform a great deal of work. Trainees often forget this and can easily slip into overtraining their arms. The long head participates in those

Figure 18.2.

movements, too, but it isn't recruited to the same degree. Most trainees follow their chest and shoulder work with direct arm work, which usually means relatively isolated arm training.

The most common triceps exercise is the pushdown, which is performed on a high cable with a straight handle, V-bar, cambered handle, rope, or single handle. The lying triceps extension has always been a popular standby. Machines that isolate the triceps are fairly common as well, and certain machines can

easily produce a triceps tendinitis—although, as you'll see, true triceps tendinitis is rare.

Kickbacks are another popular movement, while reverse dips performed with and without weight are a little less common. Considering the important role that standing and seated extensions play in triceps development, they don't seem to be used as much as they should.

Since two-joint muscles must be stretched at both joints to be maximally recruited, and the long head of the triceps is a two-joint muscle, the best exercise for the long head is one that stretches it at both the elbow and the shoulder. The standing triceps extension fills that bill. When you hold the weight over your head as if you were at the top of a military press, the long head is stretched at the shoulder but shortened by the elbow extension, or straightening. If you lower the weight behind your head, however, the long head becomes stretched at both joints. Both the shoulder and the elbow are in full flexion in that position. Remember, the long head extends the elbow and the shoulder.

Trainees used to ask the late pro bodybuilder Dave Johns how they could build their arms like his. Dave advised them to start performing the standing triceps extension for arm size. He was absolutely right. He recommended an exercise that maximally recruits the long head of the triceps, which constitutes not only the bulk of the triceps but the bulk of the arm muscles as well.

If you have lower-back pain, you may find the standing triceps extension uncomfortable to perform. In that case, try it in the seated position. Some gyms, such as World Gym in Venice, California, have a small, low-incline seat that can be placed in front of a low pulley. That works well for this exercise, especially if the pulley system is as smooth as World Gym owner Joe Gold has always made his equipment.

Note that trainees who perform the one-arm standing dumbbell triceps extension seem to complain of elbow pain more than those who use two hands on a dumbbell, barbell, or cable. I don't have an explanation for that. It's not a scientifically proven fact but, rather, observation and empirical evidence that I've come across over the past 15 years.

Once again, NABBA Mr. Universe class winner Frank Vassil demonstrates this exercise. The photos were taken at the Daniel Freeman Hospital Center for Athletic Medicine in Manhattan Beach, California. In Figure 18.1, Frank demonstrates the starting position of the standing extension; in Figure 18.2, he does the ending position, behind his head.

One key area of complaint associated with triceps training is elbow pain. I first addressed that problem in a column in the July '89 issue of *Ironman*, entitled "Triceps Training and Elbow Pain." One rarely finds a patient who has true triceps tendinitis or even triceps tendon pain; however, patients will say, "My elbow kills me when I train triceps. I must have triceps tendinitis or something." The

complaint is real, but the deduction is false. While the triceps training did cause pain, the pain comes from the forearm flexor muscles, the muscles that you work when you perform standing wrist curls.

The forearm flexor group includes both long and short muscles. The long muscles originate on the inner bony aspect of the elbow, which is known as the medial epicondyle. If you keep your wrist bent back in wrist extension during triceps training, as shown in Figure 18.3, it places a pulling-type stress on the wrist flexor muscles, which manifests itself as inflammation and pain on the inner elbow area. Such pain is usually magnified when you try to force one or two more reps on a movement such as the pushdown. The wrist is frequently allowed to bend back, or extend, when people use a fast, whipping movement to get enough momentum to finish

Figure 18.3. Don't do it this way.

an extra rep. That type of pain is commonly known as golfer's elbow—a point that's usually very annoying to advanced weight trainees who don't play golf.

In the past, the clinical name for the pain was *medial epicondylitis*, but it's more currently known as *flexor tendinosus*. Once the condition occurs, most triceps training will cause pain because the trainee doesn't correct the faulty biomechanics. Do not allow your wrists to bend back during your training. You must learn to keep your wrists straight during triceps exercises. That will prevent the undue stress on the medial epicondyle and reduce your pain.

To perform standing or seated triceps extensions, find the bar or cable attachment that works well for you. It may be a straight bar, a V-bar, a rope, or a dumbbell. That will vary from trainee to trainee. I remember hearing Arnold Schwarzenegger tell Joe Gold that he liked the subtle curve on the cambered bar as opposed to the steeper angle on other bars.

The legendary power lifter Pat Casey used to perform the standing triceps extension with more than 315 pounds. In the early 1960s, Casey also performed a bench press with well over 600 pounds. Barbarian brother David Paul performed standing triceps extensions with 315 pounds as well, and he did 5 × 520 in touch-and-go style on the bench press. I'm sure that there are quite a few trainees out there who can match those lifts but who keep it to themselves because they train for the pure joy of training and not for contests, meets, or magazines.

In short, include the standing extension in your program if you wish to add size to your arm, particularly your triceps. If you have lower-back pain, try the movement in the seated position. Keep your wrists straight to avoid or reduce the elbow pain associated with triceps training. If this is a new movement for you, start out very light and do just a few sets, maybe even 1 to start.

Two-handed dumbbell triceps extensions.

Mike Mentzer.

Chapter 19

MIKE MENTZER'S "HEAVY DUTY" TRICEPS WORKOUT

BY DAVID PROKOP

Many people feel that in 1979 and '80, Mike Mentzer was the finest bodybuilder in the world. The Pennsylvania native finished a close second to Frank Zane in the '79 Mr. Olympia, although he outweighed Zane by 30 pounds and was more defined. Then in 1980, when Arnold Schwarzenegger came out of retirement to recapture the Olympia crown in a highly controversial decision, Mentzer inexplicably placed fifth, even though he looked better than he had the previous year and was considered by most to be at least equally favored to win.

Mike, who, as a protest against what he considered corrupt judging, never competed in another bodybuilding contest after that '80 Olympia, was perhaps just as well known for his training concepts as he was for his titles. Given the quality of his physique, that's definitely saying something!

Mike's high-intensity training program, aptly named Heavy Duty, was essentially based on the exercise philosophy of Arthur Jones, the developer of Nautilus machines. According to Jones, the key to maximum muscle gains is to train intensely, not do any more sets than are minimally necessary to stimulate muscle growth, and space your workouts sufficiently so that your body has time to recuperate. In other words, train harder, train shorter, train less frequently.

It was a message that left an indelible impression on Mentzer, who was only 24 when he met Jones at the '71 Mr. America contest. Mike subsequently brought the concept to tremendous popularity in the sport—through his own bodybuilding accomplishments, which also included the '78 Mr. Universe title, earned with the first and only perfect score in history; through the accomplishments of his brother Ray, who won the '79 Mr. America using the Heavy Duty system; and through his popular Heavy Duty magazine column, his mail-order business, and his seminars.

Given the impact that the Heavy Duty concept had on the sport during that period, it's probably safe to say that if Mike Mentzer wasn't the best bodybuilder in the world in '79 and '80, he certainly was the most popular. The fact that he and Ray were the only brothers ever to become Mr. America simply added to the Mentzer mystique.

Mike started working out at the age of 12. His early inspiration was the great Bill Pearl, a four-time Mr. Universe winner.

"The guy who kept me going, the image that kept me going, the goal that I wanted to attain was that of looking like Bill Pearl," Mentzer said. "I even got my hair cut like him at one point, getting a flattop. I was especially inspired by his huge triceps, particularly when his arms were hanging down at his sides. I spent more hours than I care to admit at this

point just mindlessly gazing at Bill Pearl's arms in muscle magazines."

Indeed, the day would come when Mentzer's triceps development actually rivaled that of his boyhood idol. Mike was renowned for both his triceps and calf development, but even so, he feels that there's no doubt as to which was better.

"Yeah, I had good calves," he said, "but when I was in my best condition, my triceps were my best bodypart."

Mike trained for a couple of years on his own with a barbell set his father had bought him, but his formal introduction to weight training came when he was 14 or 15 and his father introduced him to John Myers, a local power lifter who had been working out for 10 to 15 years. As he said, "John Myers took me under his wing and taught me how to power-lift and train heavy."

They worked out three days a week with another weight lifter, Russell Hertzog, who was a regional champion in Olympic lifting and had a well-equipped home gym in his garage.

"Russell Hertzog taught me the essentials of Olympic lifting," Mentzer recalled. "And that, combined with John Myers's thrust in the area of power lifting, gave me a good, all-around base in strength training. I learned how to squat, bench-press, and deadlift and also how to do the military press, snatch, and clean and jerk. All of those things at a relatively early age helped to develop the basis of my physique."

Mike was a kid working out with two adult weight lifters, and he naturally relied on them for training guidance.

"I didn't have a clear-cut, explicit philosophy of my own at the time," he said. "I followed what was printed in the magazines, primarily the *York* magazine, which is what these guys were doing. I was influenced largely by them."

Here's the triceps routine Mike followed during the time he trained with Myers and Hertzog:

Beginning Routine
French presses
   (lying or standing)   2 × 6–8
Total sets: 2

Mike trains Aaron Baker.

French press—start.

French press—finish.

Weighted dips.

"When I first started working out with John Myers, I was training primarily as a power lifter, doing 3, 4, sometimes 5 sets per bodypart with basic exercises—squats, bench presses, behind-the-neck presses, curls, and French presses," Mentzer recalled. "Most of the training information was obtained from the *York* magazine, which was advocating much fewer sets than Weider was at the time, and I made great progress. By the time I was 15, I was squatting 500 for 2 reps and bench-pressing around 360, and I had developed a very muscular physique.

"The one direct triceps movement that John Myers had me do was one of his favorites: French presses, both lying and standing varieties, no more than a couple of sets, with fairly heavy weight done in strict form. Also, I was doing heavy bench presses for my chest, and, of course, bench presses also work the triceps. Guys who are great bench pressers and overhead pressers usually have well-developed triceps.

"And this is an important point, too, in understanding why today I limit my students to only 1 or 2 sets for triceps. I have them do bench presses and dips for their pecs before they train triceps, and those are both very direct triceps exercises."

As he said, Mike made great progress while training on the power-oriented program with Myers and Hertzog. In time, however, he went off on his own and started training at the Lancaster, Pennsylvania, YMCA, which was about 12 miles from his hometown. He was exposed to many more people and a lot of diverse training ideas, and those ideas took him offtrack.

"When I started training on my own, I took a turn in the wrong direction. I started doing many more sets. That was a mistake. My progress slowed down and at times halted. Now I understand that progress should never halt. If a bodybuilder is training with sufficient intensity and he's not overtraining, there should be an adaptive response—every time! When a person goes out in the hot August sun to get a suntan and doesn't overexpose himself, he doesn't have to go home at night and pray to God that he wakes up with a suntan.

There's an adaptive response every time. It's automatic.

"The same principle applies to exercise—and this doesn't apply just to Mike Mentzer. These are universal, objective principles of productive exercise. When the intensity of the training stimulus is sufficiently high, and you don't overtrain, and you don't train too frequently, there will always be an adaptive response; that is, you'll get bigger and stronger."

What Mike started doing for triceps at the Lancaster YMCA was what he called "the magic four."

"I did 4 sets of 3, 4, 5, sometimes even 6 exercises," he said. "Why 4 sets? I don't know. Probably because Arnold [Schwarzenegger] and Franco [Columbu] did it."

Here's a typical triceps workout from that period:

Intermediate Routine

Lying French presses	4 × 8–12
Standing French presses	4 × 8–12
Dips	4 × 8–12
Triceps pressdown	4 × 8–12
Triceps kickbacks	4 × 8–12
Total sets: 12 to 24*	

*Four sets each of 3 to 5 exercises.

"I tried everything," Mike said. "I didn't understand the nature of full-range exercise at the time. I uncritically and blindly accepted all of the doctrines and ideas printed in the magazines, because I didn't know how to critically analyze anything. I assumed that if it was printed, it had to be valid. I didn't know how to discriminate, but now I do. I've learned how to critically analyze, not just philosophical and political ideas, but training ideas. And I have no doubt—I say it unequivocally—and I can prove it to anybody open to a rational argument that Heavy Duty, high-intensity training is the only proper way to train for maximum muscle gains."

It was while Mike was still using the high-volume approach that he entered the '71 Mr. America contest, which was held, coincidentally, in York, Pennsylvania. Mentzer finished 10th behind Casey Viator, who was the first

Dip between benches—start.

Dip between benches—finish.

teenager to become Mr. America. Mike is quick to add that prior to this contest, his bodybuilding improvements had come to a virtual halt.

"I was making no further progress," he revealed. "I was doing up to 40 sets for my pecs, for instance, and I was making no progress, becoming very disenchanted and discouraged."

It was at that show that Viator introduced Mike to Jones, a meeting that revolutionized Mentzer's philosophy toward training. What Jones explained to Mike is how muscle growth occurs. One could call it the science of muscle growth.

"The volume or the duration of your training is not the most important aspect," Mentzer explained. "As a matter of fact, the duration of your training is always a negative—whether you train for a long period or a short period. Whenever you train at all, you're making inroads into your recovery ability. That's always a negative.

"The most important aspect of the workout is the intensity, which, properly defined, refers to the percentage of momentary effort you're generating. If you understand the nature of high-intensity physical training, you also know that the higher the intensity of the effort, the lesser the duration has to be—not just that it should be, but it has to be. When you're training as hard as you can, it's not that you shouldn't train long, although you shouldn't—again, because of the factor of limited recovery ability—but you can't train hard and long, for the same reason that nobody sprints for a mile! When you're running as hard as you possibly can, no holds barred, you cannot run more than 400 meters, which is why there is no 800-meter sprint. After 400 meters it becomes a middle-distance run.

"If, in fact, it were the volume of training that built muscle, the logic would have to proceed like this: If the amount of training is responsible for an individual's getting bigger and stronger, then as he got bigger and stronger, he would have to keep training longer and longer to keep getting bigger and

stronger. That's impossible because the human body possesses a limited recovery ability.

"Arthur Jones explained to me very clearly, very logically, what the science of exercise is really about. I embraced it immediately and started using high-intensity training principles. And my physique really started taking off."

Mike switched to the following triceps routine, based on his newfound philosophy, immediately after meeting Jones. It's the routine he used until he retired from competitive bodybuilding.

Advanced Routine
Superset

Nautilus triceps extensions	2 × 6–8
Weighted dips	2 × 6–8
Total sets: 4	

"I would do the Nautilus triceps extensions to failure, 6 to 8 reps, and follow that immediately—with no rest—with 1 set of heavy dips, again 6 to 8 reps. Actually, I would do 2 cycles, or supersets," Mentzer said. "If I

made one mistake in my training—and I did make more—it's that despite being the arch advocate of lesser training, I was doing too much. If I were to go back into contest training today, I wouldn't do more than 1—or at the most 2—sets per bodypart."

In making the switch to high-intensity training, Mike cut back not only on the length of his workouts but also on the frequency of training. As he put it, "I quit training six days a week for up to three hours a day. Instead, I started training 30 to 45 minutes a day three days a week. And within a short period of time after I started doing that, I won the Mr. America contest."

As Mentzer's career progressed and he became an Olympia contender, he found it advantageous to cut back on the frequency of his workouts even more. He eventually settled on an every-other-day split in which he trained half of his body on Monday, and instead of covering the other half on Tuesday, he took Tuesday off and did the second installment on Wednesday.

"Why adhere so blindly to a seven-day schedule just because we have, for matters of convenience, adopted the Gregorian calendar?" he asked. "The body's physiological processes aren't mediated by tradition. That's crap! Let's use our minds, perceive what our bodies are doing; so, I did that. And then a short time after that, there were periods where, using the same reasoning, I was still tired on Wednesday from Monday's workout, so I waited till Thursday to work out."

Mike also challenges the fact that many bodybuilders feel it's necessary to train the muscle from every angle to get complete and maximum development. This is essentially another way of saying that it's important to do a large variety of exercises, and Mentzer, as you may imagine, doesn't agree.

"I don't even think it's a valid issue," he said. "Number one, no one's ever defined the meaning of 'training the muscle at different angles.' From how many angles can you train the biceps and triceps? Hanging upside down by your feet? Doing exercises on an incline board at an infinite number of angles? What the hell does that mean, training a muscle at different angles? It's a layman's attempt—a poor attempt—at making something sound scientific when it's not.

"What is important—and this is the issue—is that weight-training exercise is about movement against resistance. Where there's no resistance, there's no exercise. A muscle has to move through its fullest range of motion against resistance.

"What I think bodybuilders mean when they talk about training the muscle at different angles is that they sense in certain exercises that the resistance drops off at a different point from where it does in some other exercises. And what they want to accomplish by doing more than one or two exercises is to provide resistance at those points in the range of motion where the first exercise didn't provide it. That's really all it is, I think. With conventional free-weight exercises, there really is no way to provide equal resistance through the entire range of motion. The only way to do it is with a Nautilus machine. The Nautilus cam was designed to provide resistance equally at all points in the range of motion. So, that ceases to be a problem."

In terms of triceps training, the fact that the triceps has three heads would, in itself, seem to imply that it takes a variety of exercises to fully develop the muscle. Or does Mike feel that you can develop all three heads just by using, say, one or two exercises?

"You can if you're providing resistance through the full range of motion and the muscle is performing all its functions. In fact, why do an exercise if it's not going to work all three heads?" he said. "Dips, which I call squats for the upper body, work all three heads of the triceps. So does the Nautilus triceps machine. Triceps pressdowns on a lat machine come close to working all three heads equally—because the exercise involves the multiple functions of the triceps, which are to extend the forearm and then bring the whole arm back and into the body. With pressdowns, you have that, and even more so with dips."

So, despite the fact that the triceps has three heads, Mike stands firm that the best way to train it is to do one exercise—or at most two. His preferences are the Nautilus triceps machine and dips. Mentzer suggests that if you don't have access to Nautilus equipment or just want a little more variety, you should do triceps pressdowns and dips, but he cautions that if you want to get the full benefits of the Heavy Duty methods he teaches, never do more than two exercises for triceps.

"I came to realize," he said, "that the issue of overtraining is the most crucial one facing most bodybuilders. And it comes down to this: If a bodybuilder performs 1 set more than the least amount required to stimulate an optimal increase in size and strength, he will not gain optimally; he may even halt progress entirely.

"And don't train too frequently. In most cases, that means not more than three times out of every seven to nine days. All of my clients are training, at the most, three days a week, and they're all making great progress."

Mike shows the importance of keeping a workout logbook.

Chapter 20

THREE HEADS ARE BETTER THAN ONE

BY T. C. LUOMA

Most people take up bodybuilding because they want to put some size on their arms. Consequently, they gravitate to biceps exercises rather than triceps movements. It's the triceps that gives the arm most of its mass, however, particularly when the arm is relaxed. Because the triceps is bigger than the biceps, it stands to reason that it requires more of a workload than does the two-headed muscle that occupies the other half of your shirtsleeve.

The beginning and intermediate routines in the following program stress proper form used in a logical arrangement of exercises. The advanced routine assumes that you've already learned proper form and focuses on improving weak points and offering specific techniques to shock your triceps into new growth.

BEGINNING ROUTINE: START OUT RIGHT—WITH YOUR ELBOWS STIFF

Here's a technique to practice in the privacy of your home that will get you ready for your first triceps workout.

Face the mirror, and with your arms hanging straight down, place your elbows next to your torso. Take a deep breath and . . . don't do anything. That's right: don't move your elbows.

I'm kidding, of course, about this being a real technique, but you get the point. Most people throw their elbows around more during a triceps workout than an NBA center does while he's coming down with a rebound. If you can remember to keep your elbows stationary, then you're most of the way there in terms of learning good form.

One of the best all-around triceps movements is the pushdown, which is done on a lat pulldown machine. Find an attachment that allows you to assume a palms-down, thumbs-in grip; in other words, a bar that is straight or only slightly angled. This kind of grip works the inner head of the triceps. To put more emphasis on the outer head, you use a rope attachment, which allows you to work with a palms-together, thumbs-up grip. Together these two variations will help you achieve complete development; however, at this stage of the game you want to alternate the two grips at consecutive workouts.

To do pushdowns correctly, stand facing the bar, and place your hands on it about nine inches apart. Lean forward slightly so that you'll be able to achieve a full contraction at the bottom without hitting your thighs. Then, without letting your elbows stray, push the bar down all the way. At the bottom of the movement, contract the muscle, and pause for a count of one or two before slowly allowing the bar to return to the starting position

Remember to use your triceps only. This is not an ab exercise, so you don't crunch your torso down, and it's not a lat movement, so you don't power the bar down with your back. Controlled cheating is permissible when you become an advanced bodybuilder, but for the time being, stick with the basics.

Although you'll eventually figure out what rep range works best for you, try 3 sets of 15 to start. A good barometer of how you're doing is if you feel a slight pump or burn in your tri's. If it doesn't feel right, try a few more reps. It sometimes takes a couple of workouts to fall into the groove.

Lying triceps extensions are often the most difficult triceps movement, because the form can be tough to master, but they're worth it because they work the entire muscle. Take a barbell or EZ-curl bar, and lie flat on your back on a bench. With the bar fully extended and your elbows locked, find your starting point by moving the bar so that it's in the same plane as your eyeballs. Once you've got it there, slide it a couple of inches toward the top of your head so that your arms are at a slight angle to the ground; you want the tension to remain on your triceps during the entire movement, even at the resting point, instead of on the bones and joints of your arms and shoulders.

That's your starting point. What you want to do is mentally freeze your elbows there. Now bend them, lowering the bar with your lower arms until it's just past the top of your head and your triceps are fully stretched. With your elbows still frozen at the same spot, raise the bar until they're locked again, mentally contract the muscle, and pause for a count of one or two, then repeat. Make sure that the

movement is slow and controlled. As with the previous exercise, 3 sets of 15 reps is a good place to begin.

Here's how the beginning triceps workout shapes up:

Pushdowns	3 × 15*
Lying triceps extensions	3 × 15

*Alternate palms-up and palms-down variations at consecutive triceps workouts.

How often should you train? Once a week is better than never, twice is better than once, and three times is usually better than twice. Any more than that, and you're pushing it. If you train consistently two or three times a week, you should be ready for the intermediate routine in about four to six months.

INTERMEDIATE TRICEPS TRAINING

Since the two exercises just described—pushdowns and lying triceps extensions—form the backbone of most triceps routines, I recommend that you continue doing them. It's time to start doing every movement to failure, however, and it's also time to add another exercise, as well as an occasional forced rep and superset. One good combination is working in some kickbacks with your pushdowns. After you do a set of pushdowns, pick up a pair of appropriately light dumbbells, and do some kickbacks. You don't want to do this superset on all three sets of pushdowns; once or twice per workout is plenty. The trick of mentally freezing your elbow in space works for this movement too. When the dumbbell is fully extended, your upper arm should be approximately parallel to your torso. In the correct position, if you were to release the dumbbell at the point of peak contraction, the weight would not go flying across the gym and hit some poor geek in the melon—it would fall straight down. So, don't use body English or momentum to fling the weight back. Kick it back slowly, using your elbow like a hinge, contract it for a count of two, and then lower it.

For added intensity, try doing the kickbacks with both arms. Although you usually

Pressdowns.

Continue until you reach failure. Again, superset the close-grip benches with your lying triceps extensions on at least one set at each triceps workout.

The third addition that I recommend for intermediate trainees is dips, a great movement that contributes to the overall mass of the triceps. I suggest, however, that you do only 1 set of 1 rep. Doesn't sound like much? Well, try it this way: With your upper body perpendicular to the ground (leaning in works the chest more) and your elbows tucked in close to your body, lower yourself as slowly as possible, even if it takes 60 seconds. Once you hit rock bottom, push yourself up again in the same manner, taking as long as you can. That's it: you're done.

At this point, your growing triceps routine lays out as follows:

Pushdowns	3 × 15*
Superset with kickbacks	1–2 × 15
Lying triceps extensions	3 × 15**
Superset with close-grip bench presses	1–2 × 15**
Dips	1 × 1

*Alternate palms-up and palms-down variations at consecutive triceps workouts.

**Or to failure.

There will come a day, most likely after you've been training for a year or two, when you just won't be satisfied with your work level, or you'll notice that your triceps have hit a plateau. When that happens, it's time to move on to an advanced routine.

FOR THE ADVANCED BODYBUILDER—HITTING ALL THE ANGLES

As with any advanced routine, your ultimate goal with your triceps training is to work the muscle beyond the pain barrier. That means forced reps, supersets, and giant sets until your triceps glow like painful cysts. It's also time to assess your weak points and correct them. For instance, if the exercises you've been doing

see people doing kickbacks one arm at a time, there's no reason why you can't bend over and work both arms together until you reach failure.

There's another effective superset that you can perform after your lying triceps extensions. Do as many extensions as possible, and then proceed immediately to a set of close-grip bench presses with the same weight. You may think that the weight you use for extensions is pathetically light for close-grip benches, but you should be so tired from the extensions that the close-grips will feel twice as heavy.

To do the close-grip presses, position your hands about five or six inches apart on the bar, and perform a standard bench press, keeping your elbows tucked in as you bench, or lower, the weight. Contract your triceps, and lower the bar until it lightly touches your chest.

One-arm pressdown—start.

If your inner triceps have failed to respond to your satisfaction, try subjecting them to some one-arm cable extensions. By assuming a thumbs-in grip and twisting your wrist until the thumb points down, you put emphasis on the inner triceps.

Aside from intensity and overcoming weak areas, the key to an advanced routine lies in using every combination of angles and exercises possible to constantly stimulate new and previously unexplored muscle fibers. What used to be just a set of pushdowns now becomes a test of will: you go to failure on the pushdowns to work the outer triceps, immediately drop the weight and go to failure using a reverse grip to hit the inner triceps, and then pick up the lower cable, gripping the rubber ball on the end, and do some cable kickbacks to work the outer, upper triceps.

Either before or after this giant set (remember, the key is to do everything differently all the time), do some dips between two benches. Instead of just using your bodyweight for resistance, pile as many 35- or 45-pound plates on your lap as possible, and crank out your reps. As you reach failure, have a partner pull off the top plate, and then keep on going. Continue in this manner until you're using just your bodyweight and you can't do another rep.

There's no end to the angles and techniques you can come up with. Just about any combination is a good one if you consistently hit different angles and you consistently feel a pump or burn after your workout. Although some people get by with as little as 9 total sets, others find that they need up to twice that number. By the time you reach the advanced level, you'll know what works best for you.

have worked for your upper tri's but not the lower portions, some partial reps may well prod the deficient area into growth.

Just about any of the exercises previously discussed will target the lower tri's if you work only through the lower range of motion. When doing pushdowns, for example, let the bar come up only one-half to three-fourths of the way before you push it down again.

One-arm pressdown—finish.

Chapter 21

HEAVILY ARMED AT HOME: TRICEPS

BY STEVE HOLMAN

The range of motion of the triceps is the same as for the biceps: upper arm next to your head, elbow bent, moving down along an arc that ends when your arm is behind your torso, elbow locked. We can construct a triceps routine that works the muscle along this range of motion. Here's the routine:

Overhead extensions*	2 × 8–10	
Close-grip bench presses	2 × 8–10	
Kickbacks	1–2 × 8–10	

*Do 2 progressively heavier warm-up sets prior to these work sets to prevent injury. This is a stretch-position movement, and because you do it first, it could cause a muscle tear if you don't warm up properly.

Notice that this routine works your triceps all along its range of motion—in other words, at points along the arc that's created when you move your upper arm from up next to your head down past your torso—the same as the range of motion of your biceps, only moving in the opposite direction.

With this routine, you train your triceps in the complete stretch position first to activate the myotatic reflex, then move to an exercise that works your tri's at a middle point along the arc of flexion. Finally, you train them at the point of maximum contraction—and there must be resistance at this point for the best results.

This routine is a variation of Positions-of-Flexion training but with a twist: you do the stretch-position exercise first, which can be more dangerous if you don't warm up thoroughly. I can't emphasize this enough. If you try this routine, be sure to do at least 2 concentrated warm-up sets prior to your first work set, and 3 warm-up sets may be even better if your triceps are completely cold.

We've had a few people here at the Ironman Training and Research Center on this program, and their arms have really blossomed—more fullness in all the heads. It's definitely a result-producing routine.

If you want to try this arm-specialization program, you can integrate it into a full-body routine, as follows:

Monday and Friday

Squats	2 × 8–10
Leg extensions	1 × 8–10
Leg curls	2 × 8–10
Standing calf raises	2 × 10–20
Seated calf raises	1 × 10–20
Bench presses	2 × 8–10
Incline presses	1 × 8–10
Pulldowns	2 × 8–10
Bent-over barbell rows	1 × 8–10
Dumbbell upright rows	2 × 8–10
Seated dumbbell presses	1 × 8–10
Lying triceps extensions	2 × 8–10
Standing barbell curls	2 × 8–10
Crunches	2 × 10–20

Wednesday

Triceps

Overhead extensions	2 × 8–10
Close-grip bench presses	2 × 8–10
Kickbacks	1–2 × 8–10

Biceps

Incline curls	2 × 8–10
Standing barbell curls	2 × 8–10
Concentration curls	1–2 × 8–10

Brachialis

Incline hammer curls	2 × 8–10

Forearms

Decline wrist curls	1 × 8–10
Decline reverse wrist curls	1 × 8–10

This allows you one day a week, Wednesday, to really bomb your arms, and then you do 2 sets each for biceps and triceps on Monday and Friday. If you find that your arms aren't responding, you may want to split the arm work over two days: train on Monday, Tuesday, Thursday, and Friday, and work the arm-specialization routine on Monday and Thursday or Tuesday and Friday.

Close grip.

Seated dumbbell triceps extensions.

INDEX